'70s Teen Pop

'70s Teen Pop

Lucretia Tye Jasmine

BLOOMSBURY ACADEMIC
NEW YORK • LONDON • OXFORD • NEW DELHI • SYDNEY

Liner Notes

Like a curious dreamer new to the experience it craves, teen pop encompasses several kinds of musical styles, not limiting itself to just one—teen pop wants to play. A subgenre of popular music, teen pop embraces other subgenres, including balladry, country, disco, glam rock, hip-hop, punk, R & B, and rock. Teen pop's play with several styles sounds like the way candy tastes: bite-sized, and in many flavors. Sometimes sweet and sometimes sour. Its lyrical insistence on self-awareness, intimate connection, rebellion and sexual respect, and its musical foundation of variety, reflects open-mindedness and multiple communities.

'70s Teen Pop provides a brief background to the origins of this subgenre of popular music, then examines how teen pop reflects evolving gender roles during the '70s, discussing how teen pop affects and is affected by the counterculture and cultural events.

This book is organized like a boom box's functions, with each section as follows: "Rewind," "Play," "Fast Forward," "Record," "Pause," and "Stop/Eject." This is because cassette tapes, mixtapes, and boom boxes were so popular in the '70s, and they signify the countercultural spirit of that decade's DIY agency. Plus, I love cassette tapes and boom boxes. "Liner Notes" is my introduction to the book. The "Rewind" section is demarcated by "Jazz and Swing," "Rock 'n Roll," "Girl Groups and Boy Bands," and "Counterculture." The "Play" section is demarcated by years: 1970–3, 1973–6, and 1976–9.

Pre-teens and teens, a market base usually unburdened by living expenses such as rent/mortgage, utilities, meals, car payments, and school loans, can spend their allowances and/or money they earn on music, movies, magazines, and comics. Portable music (vinyl, the radio, cassettes) made the universal experience feel uniquely experienced, with a sense of individual agency and ownership. Cultivation of the teen idol through radio, movies, TV shows, comics, magazines, and fan clubs contributed to a screaming, swooning, and devoted fan base. But tweens and teens bought music that wasn't primarily marketed to them, too. Music gives fans something to believe in, and something they feel is all their own.

Teen pop songs are usually about fitting in or rebelling; finding love and erotic intimacy; having fun; and developing inner strength. A longing in the songs for the mysteries of adulthood with the reassurance of intimate connection expresses an interesting combination of innocence and sophistication. The catchy music has almost always held popular sway on the radio, with periodicals and music videos offering pin-up crushes and magazine dreams in luscious visual stereo. Fashion styles, lingo, and dance moves, crucial to selling the music, signal individual identity but also community or conformity. The evolution of social construction can be seen and heard.

TV shows such as *Soul Train* (1971–2006) and movies such as Allan Arkush's musical comedy, *Rock 'n' Roll High School* (1979), demonstrate the desire to transform (and to be transformed) through music. For example, *Soul Train* shows mostly people of color dancing. Black joy—and all colorful joy—is a profound and political counter to racist culture. In *Rock 'n' Roll High School*, a groupie songwriter blows up a school to overthrow an oppressive system that denounced music. Female anger is a profound and political counter to sexist culture.

The teen idols of teen pop could be and often were role models. During the '70s, the attempt to change the status quo, understood as more difficult and taking longer than the hopefuls of the 1960s thought, can be seen in the near mythic self-presentation of some teen pop stars: Hip-hop DJs, rock's superhero make-up, and punk's torn and safety-pinned clothing are emblematic of the resourcefulness, artistry, and superhuman strength needed to make lasting change.

An example is teen pop star Cher, who influenced future countercultural legends Pamela Des Barres and Alice Bag. In the 1960s, at the cusp of Second Wave Feminism and the sexual revolution and when the term "groupie" was coined, teen-ager Pamela Des Barres joined a band called Girls Together Outrageously, or the GTOs, a troupe of seven dancing friends from California who met in the countercultural "freak scene." Pamela wrote in her diary about her experiences being a consort of rock stars and being in her own band, resulting in her bestselling memoir, 1987's *I'm with the Band*. Pamela told me that in the '60s she nicknamed her vagina "Cher" because Cher represented strength, creativity, and independence.

Alicia Armendariz from East Los Angeles started singing young. She renamed herself in 1977 when she formed her influential punk band, the Bags (featured in Penelope Spheeris's 1981 *Decline of Western Civilization*). Cher's visual presence on TV in the '70s offered an exciting reassurance to Alice Bag: people who didn't fit the beauty standard could sparkle, sing, and run their own show.

TV shows such as *The Archies*, *The Jackson 5ive*, *Josie and the Pussycats*, *The Monkees*, and *The Partridge Family* also promoted (or manufactured) musicians. An example of males as objects of desire and females with power can be seen in an episode of the popular TV sitcom, *The Brady Bunch*, "Getting Davy Jones"

(1971). Teen pop star Davy Jones from The Monkees guest appears on the show after Marcia Brady, the president of his fan club, gets him to sing at her junior prom.

Gender roles for boys and men evolved during the '70s. Male teen pop stars were portrayed in ways usually reserved for girls and women—as objects of desire, providing a space for girls and women to own and project desire rather than only reflect it. For example, SuperGroupie and super artist, Cynthia Plaster Caster, made plaster casts of musicians' penises. Hard rock teen pop band, KISS, so wished they'd been plastered that they wrote 1977's "Plaster Caster" about her (Cynthia told me she'd never cast them!).

Teen magazines such as *16*, *Right On!*, *Star*, *Teen*, *Teen Beat*, and *Tiger Beat* promoted teen pop with articles, interviews, contests, and pictorials. Centerfolds and pin-ups, however clothed or cartoonish, reframed gender roles. What had been reserved for females—sexualized poses—was opened to males: a spread that invited a reader to handle the magazine by turning it sideways in visual recline, and potentially pull out the image. Don Berrigan, *Star*'s editor and primary writer, told me, "Sometimes they'll buy the whole magazine, just for the centerfold." *Star* featured a teen pop star, David Cassidy, showering. Editorial Associate Lori Barth and legendary photographer Henry Diltz told me they were there at that shoot; they said it was good clean fun.

The teen idols of teen pop were gateway drugs. Sweet got sexy and come-ons contained a dare as individuals and popular culture dealt with admitting sexuality, confronting racism and sexism, and questioning authority. Groupies sought adventures without marriage, hip-hop handled the vinyl, punks announced an overthrow of hierarchies, and disco encouraged dancing and queer culture. Native American culture can be found in the countercultural clothing of fringe and feathers and punk's mohawk hair styles, and heard in the drumbeat and voices that sound like instruments. Teen pop, embracing many genres, challenged gender roles, racial segregation, and sexual inhibition.

Rooted in jazz and big bands, teen pop music in general offers hope: maybe individual expression can find a groove, maybe in our private longings we can find a way to play together, maybe the experience of being alive can be interpreted through a shared experience that fosters love and respect for each other, maybe the song can help us get along.

The feelings about freedom and equality that had created jazz and swing in the first place became recognized as a countercultural revolution in the '60s and could be heard in the many subgenres of teen pop during the '70s; screaming could be singing, and dancers danced without a partner. Abbey Lincoln's scream was a song in 1960's "Freedom Now Suite." Jimi Hendrix played The National Anthem on electric guitar in 1969. And Taquila Mockingbird, the singer and Punk Museum co-founder who wears floor-length couture gowns when she performs, told me jazz is "Black punk rock." Resounding the American dream of democracy and equality in a whole new way, countercultural music demonstrates that to make the American dream come true we must do it creatively.

'70s teen pop reinforced aspects of the counterculture it absorbed, working subversively as it promoted feminism, sexuality, immigration, and civil rights, challenging the status quo it seemed to represent: performers such as The DeFranco Family, Menudo, Sweet, and Andy Gibb represented various countries, and male teen idols such as The Jackson 5ive and David Cassidy posed suggestively while female stars such as Cher, Diana Ross, and Marie Osmond had their own shows.

I chose '70s teen pop to write about because I was a tween fan then, and, when I was eleven years old in 1977, wrote fantasies about the musicians. Writing fantasies was a whole new world for me, a way to experience my dreams. Writing was itself a dream coming true. In *Jazz*'s "Pure Pleasure," Duke Ellington played the piano as he told an interviewer, "This is not a piano. This is dreaming."

Teen pop is, at heart, a power ballad that wants to play, as much an expression of yearning for love, intimacy, connection, and fun as it is an expression of the struggle to establish autonomy and community, express oneself truthfully, and find meaningful purpose. *'70s Teen Pop* presses play.

Rewind

Jazz and Swing

Driving from one state to the other in the middle of the night, windows down, trying to find a station that comes in on the radio. Turning the dial, changing channels, scratchy sounds of noise and music, singers and DJs fading in and out—it sounds like its own kind of song. Then, there, distant on the dial but coming In more clearly as I drive further along, a song, a swinging song, the echoed sounds of the past bringing me here. It's Duke Ellington from 1932, "It Don't Mean a Thing (If It Ain't Got That Swing)," with Ivie Anderson singing.

Swing music swoops like an embrace that folds you in and flings you out. It sounds like freedom, and what can best be done with it—individual expression that works with others to make a song swing. It moves like laughter in a group. Ebullient, playful! I opened my window and turned up the music.

During the first half of the twentieth century in America, the unexpected sounds in jazz and the motion of swing integrated the uniqueness of individual players in the band and individual dancers on the dance floor. But stars emerged, too. Devoted fandom was cultivated through music and media, a cultivation that began with jazz musicians such as Louis Armstrong and Billie Holiday.

The Swing era foretells '70s teen pop. Swing lasted from about 1930 to 1945, ending when the singers got more popular than the big bands who played the music, soon after the end of the Second World War. The boys and men who'd gone missing in the war were made larger than life in their absence, and their stand-ins sang in swing bands. The swing singer would become a teen idol.

Dancers moved to the music daringly, making great leaps like gymnasts, literally overhead and between the legs, and around and around, with practiced and risky moves that required discipline, trust, and exploration. Dances such as the Jitterbug and the Lindy hop were wild! But in control. Like the music itself.

♥ ♥ ♥

To understand pop music, think about minstrelsy, which was popular entertainment from about 1830 to 1920. Minstrelsy developed the first pop songs as the shows went on tour across America. Minstrel shows were traveling troupes of white musicians and performers painting themselves Black who imitated Black people, especially the singing, dancing, and speaking of Black people. Sometimes, Black people dressed up as whites performing as Blacks. Minstrelsy's racism and othering allowed white people to hide their interest in Black culture in the mask of mimicry, and allowed white audiences and performers to learn about Black music and dancing.

Ragtime came from the piano-playing of African Americans in the Midwest during the late 1800s. The musicians added a syncopated rhythm to minstrel show music, African American spirituals, European folk melodies, and military marches. Itinerant musicians and the sale of sheet music spread the gospel of ragtime, as did dance orchestras.

Swing music came from jazz and ragtime. Jazz and ragtime were played in brothels, where sex was sold, and in clubs where booze was available during Prohibition (which criminalized the production and sale of alcohol from around 1920 to 1933). Jazz was improvisatory with wind instruments prominent. Ragtime was rollicking with its piano bursts and syncopated rhythm. Swing music increased the number of musicians and instruments, adding more stringed instruments and formality.

Ragtime was usually bawdy. Jelly Roll Morton (c.1885–1941), nicknamed after a perfected erotic pressure, was the first jazz composer to write his music down on paper, a piano-playing bandleader who composed jazz standards, and played his ragtime in time to what he viewed through the peephole at the brothels where he played.

Jazz began in 1800s New Orleans, a Louisiana city in Southeastern America which was a hub of cultural diversity. In 1817, enslaved people there were allowed to sing and dance on Sundays, in a place called the Congo Square. Black people, who mostly came from the West Indies, played Caribbean beats. Those beats were mixed with songs brought by Black people from the American South—spirituals, work songs, and the call and response style from the Baptist church.

Free people in New Orleans included light-skinned Black people called Creoles of Color, some of whom owned slaves. Many Creoles of Color were classically trained in music, influenced by European classical music. Free people attended the Sunday events. There was music everywhere in that parade-loving city: brass bands marching in the streets for parades, Mardi Gras, opera houses, and symphony orchestras filled the air with music.

The experience of leaving one country for another, and bringing those customs, language and sayings, food, mannerisms, dances, and clothes to a new country meant that different cultures influenced each other. Immigration to and slavery in America shaped American music.

Slavery, which began with indentured servitude over 200 years earlier, became racially based in 1661 when white servants and a Black servant ran away together. Slaves were (and are) considered property. "If you were a slave, you had to learn how to improvise," said jazz trumpeter, Wynton Marsalis, in the episode, "Gumbo," from the 2001 documentary, *Jazz*.

By the time the Civil War began in America in 1861, states were divided: The Confederacy in the South was for slavery, and the Union in the north and west was against slavery. In 1861, Louisiana seceded from the Union, but in 1862 a Federal Fleet forced their surrender. With 1863's presidential Emancipation Proclamation began the end of slavery. "The abolition of slavery made jazz music possible. It comes from a consciousness of those who are outside of something but in the middle of it," observed Wynton.

Jazz experiments with time (or beats) and dissonance (clashing or contrasting sounds), making new song structures and unexpected instrumentation, with room for improvisation, veering away from tradition. Some criticized the music for being untraditional. It's very difficult to be different in a world that shuns difference. How to be in the world of humans and their cruelly controlling codes of conduct—codes which can be found in every group of humans, however marginalized, however elevated—and manage to be yourself, and/or do what you love? It's like the history of music—songs were passed along orally, then written down, and then sometimes songs escape the confines of the page. In '70s teen pop, there were those who made great pop songs, and some of the songs experimented with structure and narrative; they were different. Some of the teen pop stars experimented with self-presentation, too.

The "big noise" of jazz sounds like a man unloosening his tie, or a woman taking off her stockings. It's the satiny swish and tumble. The term itself relates to the word "jism," or semen, an example of how language reinstates patriarchal authority, as though women's child-bearing bodies have nothing to do with spirit and the life-force. "Jazz" might also be an abbreviation of "jasmine," after the flower-based perfume that sex workers favored in Storyville, New Orleans's red-light district.

Blues also influenced pop music. Emerging from the Mississippi Delta of southern America by the mid-1800s, the blues was created by African Americans and a bent (or blue) note. With its three chords and a chorus of twelve-bar sequences, and instruments that included household items such as washboards and spoons along with more traditional instruments such as guitars and drums, the blues is secular and intimate, including call and response, hollers, shouts, and moans as well as rhymed narratives, lyrical singing of lines, and vocal intonations replacing words. The resourcefulness of instrumentation and expressive singing styles can be heard in teen pop, too.

♥ ♥ ♥

By 1901, Victrola made big business of recording music. No one had yet recorded jazz, so a listener had to be in person to hear it. By 1914, most homes had a piano, and because sheet music was sold, tunes proliferated. A listener didn't have to travel to a venue, a listener could handle the music itself by holding the page, and handling the vinyl by placing it on the turntable and cranking it up.

Louis Armstrong (1901–971), a cornetist, trumpeter, and vocalist from New Orleans, fast gained attention. He'd picked up a trumpet when he was around eighteen years old and living at an orphanage. He'd grown up in poverty but always had money in his pocket, he said, because he had "get up," selling papers, shooting dice, or hustling his music. Lil Holden, the piano player who married him, supported his music, encouraging him to be a star.

And when he joined Fletcher Henderson's band in New York, a new sound was born. It was swing, what Louis Armstong did with his trumpet, his upper lip forever changed, changing jazz. It's said he invented modern time. He broke away from Western harmony and brought forth the quarter tone. He improvised in the melody. Louis's legato was different than staccato phrasing, and he let the note stretch so that it sounded like a vocal. He added blues, and a climax, and a felt story to the sounds. His manager booked so many shows that Louis developed a callous on his upper lip that was prone to infection, and that once bled from his playing, spraying his shirt with blood during a 1933 performance.

It's also believed that Louis led the emphasis on soloists. By the 1920s, soloists became as well known as the band, taking center stage as they improvised their solos. Singers did, too, setting the stage for the teen idol. Swing got dressed up— something sexy about those touch-and-go moves in satins and dress suits, strings, and wind instruments. According to *Jazz*'s "Swing: The Velocity of Celebration," Count Basie said, "Even a single note can swing."

In 1932's "Rhapsody in Black and Blue," Louis played a minstrel song with the orchestra behind him on a stage filled with bubbles and glitter. He wore animal prints and silver sparkles, moving gracefully, making me think of '70s Glam Rock. Louis seems like a teen pop idol to me. I think Louis Armstrong is the first real pop star.

He recorded his scat singing, or when he would "hum like an instrument," according to *Jazz*'s "Our Language," replacing words with vocal intonations. When he performed Fats Waller and Harry

Brooks's "Ain't Misbehavin'" at the all-Black revue, "Hot Chocolates" in 1929, the audience got so excited they cheered him from the orchestra pit to the stage. Fans copied his white handkerchief, his vocabulary, and his voice. He reportedly was the first to call someone a "cat," and to refer to musical skills as "chops."

His influence on popular culture is so enduring that, in 1964, he became the oldest artist to ever hit number one when his version of "Hello, Dolly" pushed The Beatles out of the number one slot on the Billboard chart. In the '70s, as a young girl, I imitated his voice when I sang because I liked its gravel. Within his resonant and varying intonations, he sounded fun.

Someone else I loved in the old-time cinema I watched as a kid was elegant Duke Ellington (1899–1974) from Washington, D.C. In 1927, the composer, whose orchestra found steady work at The Cotton Club where only white audiences were allowed, was the first Black bandleader who had national airtime on the radio. Ivie Anderson (1904–49), a Californian known for her jazz phrasings, bluesy feeling, and scat singing, joined Duke Ellington's orchestra in 1931, and sang with them for the next eleven years. When she sang with Anson Weeks at the Mark Hopkins Hotel in San Francisco in 1928, she may have been the first Black singer to perform with a white orchestra.

Duke was so admired that in 1929 Hollywood built a film around him, *Black and Tan*, and in it he played his 1927 "Black and Tan Fantasy," an homage to the clubs where people of different colors mingled and danced together. His music was called "jungle music" because of its atypical harmonies and original chords (or combinations) and key changes.

In 1929, the stock market crashed and the Great Depression began. The Jazz Age ended. Records were burnt to keep beggars warm, and most record companies folded. The Victor Company sold radios instead of record players; radio was free for listeners. Fats Waller earned so little for his songs that he sold them twice.

And when Prohibition ended in 1933, people drank at home; people couldn't much anymore afford the clubs. Radio was the least expensive mass medium for music, and radio created stars. "The radio was like a religion," teen pop idol, Frank Sinatra, remembered. "They were even shaped like cathedrals." Popular music emerged as commercially driven music heard by many people. Teen culture emerged through the marketing of music; teens bought records, too.

It's believed that the first teen pop idol was Bing Crosby (1903–77) from Washington state. Bing wanted to be like Al Jolson (1886–1950), a Russian Jewish man from Lithuania who performed in blackface for 1927's *The Jazz Singer*. The movie introduced white audiences to Black music in one of the first films to synchronize talking, dialogue, and music to moving image. Bing Crosby also performed in blackface—in the 1943 film, *Dixie*.

Jazzy Bing with the sleepy eyes and a lazy bedroom manner is often considered the first teen pop idol because of the following: he was everywhere on the radio and on the covers of magazines; his 1941 song, "White Christmas," written by Irving Berlin, sold more than any other album; and he was a white man with a sultry slant to his profile, just sexy enough to be interesting but suited enough to be safe, his short hair slicked back, and his casual-wear somewhat dressy (jackets and ties and slacks, a tilted hat). Bing with his pipe, watch, and hat looked like laid-back authority. According to the 2015 documentary, *Sinatra: All or Nothing At All*, Bing was the first white singer who internalized jazz rhythms through his listening to Louis Armstrong.

♥ ♥ ♥

By the mid-1920s dancehalls and speakeasies were plentiful, dance bands toured and there were all-female orchestras, such as the Darlings of Rhythm, the Darling Saxophone Four, Helen Lewis and Her All-Girl Jazz Syncopators, the International Sweethearts of Rhythm (which was among the first integrated bands), the Parisian Redheads, and the Prairie View Coeds. But so many bands were named after the male bandleaders, and not the women singing for them or the musicians in the orchestra, indicating the hierarchy of labor.

The music inspired new dances, such as the Turkey Trot and the Shim Sham Shimmy. These dances required an energetic exuberance that can be seen as a rebellion against the corseted Victorian Era of the 1800s. I tried a few of the moves to see how it felt to do them, and, after a few unsure steps, the playfulness made me laugh! Making me think of Freddie Keppard who made his coronet laugh. The terrifying liberation of Modernism in a newly godless world! As the scientific analysis of the Enlightenment became a viable counterpart to religion's variables, music became the new divinity, with dance an expression of freedom, and singers the new idols.

Solo instrumentalists were popular. Sidney Bechet (1897–1959), a clarinetist born in New Orleans, introduced the soprano saxophone to jazz. Johnny Hodges (1907–70) was an alto saxophonist whose sexy swaggering sounds a lot like slowed down rock 'n roll. Big bands typically had three sections: the reeds (such as clarinet and saxophone), the brasses (such as trumpet and trombone), and the rhythm section (piano, bass, drums). Sometimes, big bands were four-piece, adding guitar or banjo. Big bands originated with usually ten players in the early 1900s as ensembles for dancers, and they played mostly improvisatory jazz, but by the 1940s swing was the thing, and the number of musicians in big bands increased to sometimes more than double. Riffs began as a call-and-response between the band and the solo, and riffs were repeated to hypnotic effect. The call and response of big bands was like the call and response in Baptist churches.

Swing music reportedly saved the record industry. By the late 1930s, big band swing created 70 percent of the music industry's profits. In 1932, ten million records were sold, but by 1939, fifty million records were sold! There were ballrooms in many cities for the big bands of swing and those who danced to them, or went to listen. In 1938, swing even played Carnegie Hall, such was its popularity.

Wynton Marsalis, in *Jazz*'s "Pure Pleasure," pointed out that "the flowering of the American popular song" was nurtured by big bands with lots of material to play. Faith in an adult sensibility and a belief in America combined with jazz's joy, the prevalence of clubs, and the radio contributed to the popularity of big bands.

Some of the most popular bandleaders were Black, like Jimmie Lunceford and Willie "the Lion" Smith. Some were Jewish. Benny Goodman (1909–86), the son of Jewish Russian immigrants, learned the clarinet and became one of the first bandleaders with an integrated orchestra. And there were women bandleaders, too—Lil Hardin Armstrong (who married Louis), Blanche Calloway (older sister of Cab) and her Joy Boys (what a name!), and Thelma White. The Second World War was about ethnic cleansing, and when America joined the war against it, American swing music represented that democratic, participatory, and open spirit of freedom even as it represented the struggle to get there. "Swing has a marvelous thing of bringing people together," said professional dancer, Norma Miller in *Jazz*'s "The True Welcome."

Dancing was so continuous that the mahogany floor had to be replaced at the Savoy every three years. Drummer and bandleader Chick Webb (1905–39) had his drums nailed to the floor, that's how hard he kickpedalled! He and Benny Goodman had a throw-down concert competition in 1937 at the Savoy, with 4,000 people in attendance—and 5,000 more who couldn't get in the club! Benny's drummer, Gene Krupa, said Chick "cut me to ribbons."

When Benny Goodman and His Orchestra toured out of their own pockets in 1935, concerts weren't popular. At one show, they played behind chicken wire as they were pelted (like a '70s punk rock show!). But when they arrived in Los Angeles to play the Paloma, a venue where teens were allowed, the band was met by a throng. On March 3, 1937, Benny Goodman and his swing band performed a two-week engagement at the Paramount Theater in Times Square, Manhattan, and the joint was mobbed. High school students danced in the aisles and sometimes on the stage. Gene Krupa's hair was unleashed from its oiled styling as he played the drums, swinging like his music, during the 1936 Louis Prima song, "Sing Sing Sing (with a Swing)" establishing the drummer (and the drum solo) as an exciting star—and the instrumentalist as romance object.

Another new solo star from Benny's band was the guitar. Charlie Christian's amplified guitar playing made a guitar solo equivalent to the clarinet, trumpet, or saxophone solos. This predicts the guitar swagger of music in the '70s.

"Swing music was an electrifying development in American popular culture. It unleashed forces that I think people didn't know existed," said music critic Gary Giddins in *Jazz*'s "Swing: Pure Pleasure." "It was just fun to get up and move with that beat," said club owner Lorraine Gordon. Gary also said that swing was Louis Armstrong orchestrated.

♥ ♥ ♥

Adults were fans of swing music, but it was the teens who made it swing nationally, according to *Jazz*'s "Swing: Pure Pleasure." There was a look to go with the sound: saddle shoes with bobby sox for girls, who wore pleated skirts that could flare when they danced, and sports jackets and loose slacks for boys. Trumpet and clarinet sales increased. Bandleaders had fan clubs and love letters with phone numbers. Some bandleaders were frightened by the fans, such as Benny Goodman, and some were contemptuous, such as Artie Shaw. Gary Giddins likened the bandleader to a rock star.

Teen girls swooned when Frank Sinatra (1915–98), a blue-eyed crooner known as "The Voice," sang with swing bands. The fans became as famous as the heartthrob: known as "bobbysoxers," their being named indicates a recognition of the fans' importance. Bobbysoxers demonstrate the emergence of teen pop as a genre, with tweens and teens being seen as real people with significant impact and cultural clout; their opinions mattered.

Bobbysoxers were so named because of the socks they wore. Silk and nylon were rationed during the Second World War, so suppliers made a short nylon sock. If those weren't available, white socks were cuffed above the shoes, usually black and white saddle shoes, ballet slippers, or penny loafers. Pants or jeans were rolled up to showcase the white anklets, or bobby socks. And so the socks teen girls wore were related to war, swing, rebellion, and rock 'n roll.

More teens attended high school by the 1940s, so it makes sense that a teen market emerged then, too. *Seventeen* magazine was launched in 1944, influencing readers by showcasing styles. When I was twelve in 1978, I read teen magazines that showed models wearing bobbysox with sandals, showing the far reach of style over generations.

A star text is a story told about an artist that differs from the true story, intended to create a mystique or persona. Were the bobbysoxers born from star text? According to writer, Lee Server, original bobbysoxers at the Paramount Theater show were paid to scream and faint by George Evans, Frank Sinatra's personal publicist, "causing by example a legendry riot of unhinged swooning in the theater and miles of subsequent press attention."

But in the 2015 documentary about Frank, a bobbysoxer remembers what it was like. "That was the thrill of our life. We used to go there, 35 cents, sat there all day, we were poor but we always had money to go to the Paramount and see Sinatra. When he'd walk out, and then the band would play the intro to his songs, oh, you'd get goosebumps," remembered Rose Cafasso.

Frank wanted to be more popular than Bing Crosby. Born to Italian-Jewish parents who immigrated to America, Frank Sinatra knew from racial slurs against his heritage. Italians were sometimes lynched in America. Frank was put down by other kids for the facial scarring he retained from his difficult birth. This vulnerability can be heard in his singing, a vulnerability that made him a target for derision—but also desire. Frank took vocal lessons, learning how to sing slowly (and safely, so his vocal chords would be intact).

The slow swing of big band ballads made room for dancing and romance. Frank Sinatra's vocals sound almost lonely amidst the big band sound surrounding him, sincere and romantic and emotionally heroic. His recording of 1939's "All or Nothing at All" with Harry James and his orchestra was not a hit at first, but a reissue during the Musician's Strike in 1943 made it so. His tempered vocals make romantic command of erotic urgency, an old-fashioned sexiness whose persuasive expression many found impossible to resist. A listener can tell he is really thinking about the words he sings as he sings them.

Shrewd Frank! Figuring out how to release his music during a music strike (by releasing music that he'd recorded before the strike), and figuring out how to magnify his sex appeal (by his use of a microphone). Although he'd sung with a megaphone like early teen idol, Rudy Vallée (1901–86), to project his voice, Frank significantly invested in a microphone. The microphone amplified a vocal intimacy. When Frank sang with Tommy Dorsey's orchestra, the audience crowded the bandstand to listen to him sing, rather than dance. "It was pandemonium all the time. Chaos," observed his daughter, Nancy in the documentary. "The kids would scream every time I came out on the stage," remembered Frank. His way of dropping a note in the word he sings added emotional weight. He publicly credited cabaret singer, Mabel Mercer (1900–1984), with his own style, appreciating her talking style of singing.

♥ ♥ ♥

The subjective self of Modernism took center stage with the soloist amidst sounds that began with the jazz ensemble, which let different players move in different directions, a dissonance that sounded and felt good, but a sound that threatened the prevailing status quo. The frenetic quality of the new century heralded the propulsive soundtrack of industry. Swing soothed and exalted during Depression era and wartime. The bands would rise up from the stage, thrillingly revealed bit by bit, in dress-up clothes that seemed glamorously unified.

Vocalist Billie Holiday (1915–1959) sang just behind the beat with her one-octave voice, creating her own musical phrases. She considered herself a musician. By age twelve, she sang along to the Victrola for extra money in the house that employed her as a sex worker, and by age thirteen, she'd moved to New York where she sang at jam sessions and rent parties, and at eighteen, she recorded with Benny Goodman. In 1937, Count Basie hired her, whose sideways-playing saxophonist, Lester Young, nicknamed her "Lady Day." Billie sang "Strange Fruit," a poem set to music written by Abel Meeropol, a song whose explicit politics expressed a militancy and a protest, commented Gerald Early in *Jazz*'s "Swing: The Velocity of Celebration."

Songs could express motivational solidarity. The Andrews Sisters in a 1941 Abbott and Costello movie, *Buck Privates*, sang "Boogie Woogie Bugle Boy," an upbeat jump blues song written by Don Raye and Hughie Prince about a soldier dedicated to music. Contralto LaVerne (1911–67), soprano Maxene (1916–95), and mezzo Patty Andrews (1918–2013) were born in Minnesota to immigrant parents (their dad was from Greece and their mom from Norway), and the sisters began their career performing on the vaudeville circuit. Their first hit in 1937 was a Yiddish tune, "Bei Mir Bistu Shein," with a Germanized title, "Bei mir bist du schön." It's bawdy without being vulgar, it's sung by women, and they are not ashamed to admit erotic experience.

Each language only helps me tell you how grand you are

is a line that I love because it suggests cross-cultural influences, which is the heart of music. Plus, it's a loving (and possibly sexy) line. But because the publishing rights were sold before the song's success, and it was rewritten, the original composer, Sholom Secunda from Russia, and lyricist, Jacob Jacobs, from Hungary, did not receive as much profit as the song warranted, and the singing sisters didn't get the royalties, an example of how art is an ideal we often only reach in the expression of the art itself.

And then there are ideals that aren't inclusive. Ella Fitzgerald (1917–96) was a teen-aged numbers runner and a lookout for brothels after dropping out of high school. In 1934, wearing a pair of men's boots and a secondhand dress, she won First Prize during amateur night at the Apollo, which promised a week-long engagement. But the engagement was denied to her because the club's manager thought she wasn't pretty enough. By 1936, when she was recruited for Chick Webb's band, Chick said about Ella, "You're not putting that on my bandstand," according to *Jazz*'s "Swing: The Velocity of Celebration." But singer Charles Linton said he'd quit Chick's band if Ella wasn't hired. And then: at nineteen years old, she was billed the First Lady of Swing. She also became friends with Chick, and after he died in 1939, his band became her band—and she renamed it with her own name. Ella could scat (that singing style without words), she experimented with Be Bop (experimental jazz), and she created pop ballads.

Ballads by the Ink Spots were popular in the 1930s and 1940s. Their high tenor vocal among layered backing vocals presaged doo-wop, the singing style popularized on street corners during the 1950s. Their guitar riffs influenced R & B as well as rock 'n rollers. The sincerity of their 1939 "If I Didn't Care" can be heard in Elvis Presley's vocal delivery, with its Top & Bottom, or "talking bass" style, which is singing followed by spoken words. Interestingly, the seriousness sometimes veers into a hint of mockery in balladeers, a mockery that pop stars in the '70s endured as their own music was used against them.

♥ ♥ ♥

Despite Sinatra's popularity, the ballads and dance songs of swing weren't embraced by everyone. Swing was also criticized: as being aggressive and sexual, as a narcotic, and as a distraction.

And racial segregation barred people of color from convenient lodging, food, and places to bathe and use the restroom. In 1933, Blacks were only allowed in the balconies, and Black bandleaders and orchestras were barred from white restaurants and hotels. So Duke Ellington and his orchestra toured in their private Pullman cars (sleeping cars that moved along railroads). When asked about it, Duke said they were traveling like the president.

During the Depression, earning too little as a musician would be better than earning nothing. It's disheartening to realize the democracy jazz represents is also troubled by competing soloists, unequal pay, and oppressive (band) leaders—the hurt inherent in hierarchies. Bandleader Benny Goodman reportedly ripped off royalties, and bandleader Duke Ellington reportedly pitted players against each to get a better performance from them. Popular bandleaders could make a lot of money. And the music represented and provided so many things at once.

Anita O' Day, the jazz singer who began performing as a teen and who challenged gendered expectations by wearing shorter skirts and a jacket onstage, sang with Roy Eldridge (a trumpeter who learned drums at six years old), in one of the first recorded interracial duets for 1941's "Let Me Off Uptown." The song was a hit but racist club policy prevented them singing side by side, and racist hotel policies prevented him having a place to stay.

Benny Goodman was made fun of for his Jewish heritage. Artie Shaw changed his name from Arthur Jacob Arshawsky. In Germany, jazz was called "nigger jew music." By 1943, the word "jazz" was banned in occupied Europe. But rebellious youth in Germany known as "swing kids" met in secret to listen to swing and dance to it, and Parisians simply changed the words to hide the kind of music they danced to and loved. Swing, born from jazz, carries its essence. "Jazz expresses the hope of a free people who hunger for a better life. It is based on individuality, which is contrary to the very fundamentals of Naziism," said Earl Hines in *Jazz*'s "Dedicated to Chaos."

Meanwhile: in America, internment camps from 1942 to 1945 separated anyone with at least 1/16th Japanese heritage from Americans (Japan was on Germany's side). Guards sometimes killed the prisoners, as when older people struggled to march or when people walked too close to the barbed wire enclosure. And then, the Korean War, from 1950 to 1953, caused more deaths and physical suffering in a shorter time than other wars. It's considered a "hot war" during the Cold War because of the physical fighting. Swing got regimented and commercial. What would happen to the music that began as rebellious joy?

Rock 'n Roll

Sister Rosetta Tharpe's "Rock Me" from 1938 sounds like prayer with a beat. The guitar-wielding singer born Rosetta Nubin (1915–1973) from Arkansas went on tour with her mom and an evangelical group when she was six years old after picking up a guitar at age four, and she played with swing and jazz bands during the '30s and '40s. Her 1944 "Strange Things Happening Every Day" rocks gospel with its jaunty piano, guitar gallop, and cheerful chorus, an African American spiritual that is the basis of rock 'n roll.

Rock 'n roll added a jump to the blues, a country twang, the most melodious excerpts from jazz, and a gospel to swing, combining it all in usually short and danceable songs. Television promoted the new genre.

During the late 1940s and early 1950s, televisions proliferated and so did airtime as the FCC (Federal Communication Commission) rulings changed to allow more stations. Media moguls consolidated power by buying up airtime and publications, or creating new ones such as *TV Guide*, telling viewers what to watch when.

American Bandstand was a TV series that aired from 1952 to 1989. Originally a television show in Philadelphia hosted by radio disc jockey, Bob Horn, its first guest was jazz musician, Dizzy Gillespie. In 1956, middle-aged Bob was replaced by the youthful (and younger) Dick Clark, who looked more like the teens on the show. *Bandstand* changed its name to *American Bandstand* and added color cameras when it went national in 1957. It was live five days a week until 1963, and then it went to weekly pre-records, or tapings. At first, the show included teens of color and music made by people of color. But over time, a dress code and an invitation-only policy excluded teens of color until 1964. Lyrical content could be brazen but slow dancing, and especially slow dancing of mixed races, was not allowed. Dancing reflects politics.

Born in 1929, Dick Clark cultivated a sophisticated wholesomeness that became a hallmark of teen pop until the '70s. His look was clean-cut with his short hair and dressy attire, his demeanor polite. Nicknamed the "world's oldest teen-ager," he seemed casually formal. Teens sat on bleachers when they weren't dancing, and Clark sat next to them on the bleachers, handing them the mic so they could rate the songs and say what they thought of the song. Musicians performed, and teen dancers signaled trends with their fashion and dancing styles. The show presented the importance of a teen-ager's opinion. The show's power—and Clark's influence—created teen idols like Fabian and Paul Anka.

During the 1950s and early 1960s, teen idols such as Frankie Avalon, The Beach Boys, The Everly Brothers, and Bobby Rydell also tidied up the clamor of music (and bodies) that could careen out of control. Their short hair and inviting smiles! Their formality appealingly casual! Their music telling stories of romance! Pop music became a shorthand for the short and formulaic songs that would eventually create '70s teen pop. But The Beach Boys, with their surf culture and weirdly cool harmonies, and Bobby Rydell, with his bad boy pompadour, suggested the coming counterculture, and the variety of '70s teen pop.

Ricky Nelson was one of the first to utilize television as a way to promote his music, and is another singer often cited as the first teen pop idol. Born in 1940 in New Jersey, his parents met in a band: his mom was the vocalist and his dad the bandleader. Ricky co-starred on his parents' TV show, *The Adventures of Ozzie and Harriet*, a half-hour comedy drama that aired from 1952 to 1966, one of the longest running TV programs. The TV show began in 1944 as a radio program, which Ricky and his older brother David appeared on in 1952, replacing the actors who'd played the siblings. Shot in black and white until 1965, and written by their bandleader father, Ozzie, *The Adventures of Ozzie and Harriet* was about the brothers' relationship, and the raising of a family to raise more families. In the TV series, the younger son becomes a teen-aged musical sensation.

Ricky reportedly detested his 1958 hit, "Poor Little Fool," a song written by seventeen-year-old Sharon Sheeley (who wrote it upon finding out her older lover, pop star Don Everly of The Everly Brothers, was married), and refused to sing it on the show. But it became a number one hit single with the croon of his voice cradled by a chorus and a slowed down country rock. Ricky, who'd learned drums from jazz musician Louis Bellson, liked rock 'n roll and rockabilly better.

The Adventures of Ozzie and Harriet promoted Ricky's songs and created a pop star narrative that encouraged the idolization of musicians. Ricky sang ballads in the early years, but wanted to try new things. In 1962, Rick charted with "Teen Age Idol," an understated song whose title reinforced his teen idol status and the romanticization of the lonely star (and which was covered by rock drumming legend, Keith Moon, in 1975, and by punk band, The Vandals, in 1991), but by then he'd dropped the youthful "y" from his name, trying to form his own identity. By the late 1960s, the TV show had ended, and Rick formed the Stone Canyon Band and they played country rock even after his fans didn't like it, illustrating the struggle to grow up into personally satisfying musical autonomy, a struggle shared by idols such as Artie Shaw, Elvis, and David Cassidy.

Similar to jazz and swing, rock 'n roll was amplified by women and people of color. LaVern Baker (1929–97), one of the first rock 'n roll stars, had a hit with 1954's "Tweedlee Dee," a song that sounds like early rock 'n roll with its fun beat and nonsense words. A Black woman singing to a Latin beat points to the merging of diverse cultures and regions in American music. Her "Jim Dandy" from 1956 is credited with shaping rock. Pianist and singer, Ray Charles, combined jazz and blues with gospel in his rocking music for a sound people called soul, or rhythm and blues, and teen-agers loved it.

Teens were centerstage: Frankie Lymon was twelve when he joined a doo-wop group most famously known as Frankie Lymon and the Teenagers. Everyone in the band was a teen-ager—two of its founding singers met in a Manhattan high school. Frankie's vocals were searing and soaring, his smile playful, mischievous, and cute. They signed with Gee Records after the success of 1956's "Why Do Fools Fall in Love?" The band's name, the record label's name, the youthfulness of Frankie's voice, and the teen-agers in the band signify an investment in and an identity of a musical genre meant for—or claimed by—young people. A teen idol who actually was a pop and R & B star for the entirety of his teens, Lymon died before he got old, of a heroin overdose at age twenty-five in 1968.

Annette Funicello, herself a 1950s teen idol, was written about by another teen idol, Paul Anka, with his 1959 single "Puppy Love." Annette got her start on *The Mickey Mouse Club*, a variety show that ran from 1955 to 1959, and that has aired off and on ever since, making more teen pop stars. The show featured teen-aged entertainers called Mouseketeers who sang and danced and performed in skits, a show whose young stars would codify teen pop at the end of the century.

Bands such as the Champs, The Coasters, the Del-Vikings, The Diamonds, Fats Domino, The Flamingoes, The Platters, and The Weavers made songs that were popular, and singers such as Pat Boone, Patsy Cline, Sam Cooke, Mario Lanza, Brenda Lee, Johnny Mathis, Debbie Reynolds, Neil Sedaka, and Jackie Wilson also further signaled the racial and gender diversity on the pop charts during the 1950s and 1960s. Genres separated by skin color—race records that became rhythm and blues that became rock 'n roll—instilled an aural segregation enacted by laws and cultural codes, but the music invited us all to play and dance together, an invitation sent out by '70s teen pop, too.

Although the phrase "rock 'n roll" was probably old slang for sex in Black communities, a white DJ, Alan Freed, was credited with coining the term. Alan had televised dance shows where the dancing was desegregated, and spun vinyl by Black artists. Like many DJs of this era, he got into trouble for payola, the illegal practice of pay for play. That didn't diminish his enormous influence, however.

Pioneering musician Chuck Berry alludes to the power of the DJ in his 1956 "Roll Over Beethoven," illustrating his own emerging power as a Black man in white society:

> Well, I'm a write a little letter
> I'm gonna mail it to my local DJ

because Chuck has a record he wants to hear on the radio. But around this time, as diverse races were making rock 'n roll music, whites were increasingly identified as the makers of this new genre. "Rock Around the Clock," a song sung by Bill Haley & His Comets, equated white skin with rock 'n roll when it played in 1955's film, *Blackboard Jungle*, which tells the story of a teacher nicknamed Daddio by students at the inner-city school where he teaches. Bill Haley, a former country singer, was white.

"Rock Around the Clock" reached the top of the charts after *Blackboard Jungle*. The 1956 film, *Rock Around the Clock*, capitalized on the popularity of the song, and the rock 'n roll genre of music, with a storyline about how big band music is dead and a new kind of music is heralded by a local band—Bill Haley & His Comets.

Legend has it that the music in *Blackboard Jungle* inspired teen moviegoers to slash up the movie seats and riot. A few years later, Link Wray & His Ray Men released 1958's "Rumble," the only instrumental ever to be banned because the guitar sounded so … provocative. Improvised for a popular dance called The Stroll and based on a song by The Diamonds, the song sounds like it's saying "get ready." This embodiment of teen life reminds me of the energy of dancing.

Sock hops in the 1950s were dances in gymnasium. Teen dancers took off their shoes and danced in their socks so they wouldn't scuff the floor, dancing to rock 'n roll instead of swing. Dances such as the Stroll, the Hand Jive, the Cha Cha, and the Jitterbug (which was based on swing's Lindy Hop) were popular. Jukeboxes were filled with 45s of rock 'n roll. Introduced to the market in 1949, 45s were records that played up to five minutes per side, long enough for a song. With an adaptor for the center hole, listeners could spin the vinyl or polystyrene at home on their own turntables, too.

Fast tempo songs and ballads were the most popular songs during the '50s and '60s. A young piano player from South Carolina, Chubby Checker (b 1941), popularized a dance move with his 1960 cover song, "The Twist," originally played in 1959 by The Midnighters. Merchandise such as chewing gum, t-shirts, ties, dolls, and even raincoats promoted the teen singer and the song. The dance involved twisting your body while planting your feet, and did not require a partner or any touching.

Chuck Berry's duck walk as he modified a blues beat to songs about teen life, and Jerry Lee Lewis's boogie-woogie gospel piano-playing that got so raucous he played the keys with his feet, his elbows, and his backside, energized audiences. Chuck's 1964 "No Particular Place to Go" especially conveys teen life with its freewheeling optimism and sense of humor (in a car with time to spare, a stuck safety belt, and pretty colors all around).

The codification of rock as white heterosexual male was terrifically and consistently interrupted by a musician who confounded gender roles: Richard Wayne Penniman (1932–2020) from Macon, Georgia. He performed as Little Richard, calling himself the King of Rock—and the Queen. His "A-wop-bop-a-loo-bop-a-lop-bam-boom" may be the first true call to rock 'n roll, from 1955's "Tutti Frutti," which he wrote. His rambunctious piano playing and his hollers (inspired by Louis Jordan and also by The Famous Ward Singers, led by Clara

Ward) make a god time—I mean, a good time—of his gospel-infused and rollicking dance songs, many of which he wrote, including 1956's "Long Tall Sally" and 1957's "Lucille."

As rock 'n roll evolved, some performers added country to the mix, such as Elvis Presley. The boy who flunked music in high school but who sang at home with his parents became an icon, and one of the top-selling musical artists of all-time. His teen pop idoldom is monumental.

Elvis Presley was born in a two-room shotgun house in Tupelo, Mississippi, 1935. A twin brother died at birth, and his mom, Gladys, told him if he sang to the full moon his brother would hear him. When Elvis was thirteen, the family moved to Memphis, Tennessee, and into a housing project funded by the New Deal, programs designed to stabilize people during the Depression. Beale Street in Memphis was alive with gospel and country music played by Blacks and whites.

He dyed his blonde hair black because he thought it made him look more glamorous, and he wanted to join a gospel quartet like The Blackwood Brothers. Sam Phillips at Sun Records pulled his voice in close to the music, not out front like Frank Sinatra's but close to the instruments playing.

Sam wanted to bring the Black sound to a white audience, which they did, with Elvis's 1954 recording of "That's All Right," originally written and recorded in 1946 by Arthur "Big Boy" Crudup, who borrowed a few lines and traditional blues verses from Blind Lemon Jefferson's 1926 "That Black Snake Moan." Elvis combined bluegrass with blues.

Elvis stuttered on his first radio interview, but the vocal stutter in his songs is recognized as a vocal technique. DJ Dewey Phillips was flooded with phone calls off the hook in Memphis after playing Elvis on air. The sound of the music was stripped down and bare, with Scotty Moore on guitar, Elvis on acoustic rhythm guitar and vocals, and Bill Black on an upright string bass, which Bill slapped for the drum sound, combining blues and country with gospel for a new pop sound. In concert, Elvis's charismatic appeal as he grabbed the mic and dragged it across the stage made the performance of music sexual—the physicality of romance as it moved from emotion and thought to physical expression.

After a 1956 appearance on *The Ed Sullivan Show*, Elvis was burned in effigy. He was televised from the waist up for *The Ed Sullivan Show* in 1957. "If you see a large social anxiety on the horizon, there's probably issues of bodies and control involved," comments the writer Warren Zanes in *Elvis Presley: The Searcher*. Elvis's music—and how Elvis sang it—meant males could dance sensually and females could desire.

> Young people, whether they were physically mixing Black and white or not, they were culturally mixing Black and white the way they were expressing themselves. The movements in space as that mixing happened were sexual in nature. And I think with the case of Elvis—the fearful response, it had a racial component, and a sexual component. You know, it's all about fear and the body.

Elvis's music was put down with racial slurs because his sound was based on Black music.

In *Black Diamond Queens: African American Women and Rock and Roll* (2020), scholar and author, Maureen Mahon, says that Elvis "produced a Black sound, drawing his predominantly white audiences into a sonic experience whose overt racial mixing was at once enticing and illicit." In *The Story of Rock: Smash Hits and Superstars*, Elvis is quoted: "Rock and roll has been around for many years. It used to be called rhythm and blues." R & B was Black music.

The hip-swinging singer known as Elvis the Pelvis sang "Peace in the Valley" on *The Ed Sullivan Show* too, a gospel song, because it was his mother's favorite song. Gospel music soothed him, and Elvis played it privately the night he died, in 1977, from prescribed medication.

"Front man is something that was derived from preacher fronting the choir in church," observed Bruce Springsteen in *Elvis Presley: The Searcher*. "So whether you're James Brown or Elvis or anyone out there your position basically is always proto-religious." Elvis combined sexual charisma with religious fervor, the alchemy creating a pop star idoldom.

Maureen Mahon also points out that by the late '60s, Elvis was performing with the Sweet Inspirations as backup, demonstrating "his reliance on, regard for, and debt to Black women's vocal sound, on stage and on record." Elvis hired the Sweet Inspirations in 1969 without auditioning them. The vocal group, who had sung back up for Aretha Franklin and Otis Redding, included Cissy Houston, the mom of eventual superstar singer, Whitney Houston. The Blossoms sang the backing vocals for 1968's "If I Can Dream." Singer, Darlene Love, told the *Village Voice* that he paid them well and treated them with respect.

Elvis also employed white gospel singers such as the Stamp Quartet and the Voice as back up. White women who sang back up for Elvis over the years included Millie Kirkham and Kathy Westmoreland. In footage of concerts from the '70s, Black and white singers are onstage singing with Elvis. His desire to truly work with the band with whom he shares the stage a desire one can actually see and hear in concert footage. The combined sound was immense.

It sounded as though races could successfully mix. There were popular bands in the '70s that were integrated, such as Sly and the Family Stone and KC and the Sunshine Band. Leon & Mary Russell released *The Wedding Album* in 1976, and the album cover showed that he was white and she was Black. Similarly, '70s teen pop included music made by diverse groups.

Girl Groups and Boy Bands

Girl groups emerged in the late 1950s to the early 1960s, their harmonizing based in doo-wop and gospel, their pop arrangements marketable and popular. Groups such as The Angels, The Crystals, the Shirelles, the Supremes, and Martha and the Vandellas were high on or topping the popular charts. Glamorous and unified clothing onstage and dulcet tones in catchy melodies provided a disciplined formality that sometimes hinted at the wild in groups such as the Shangri-Las, clearly heard in their teen tragedy tune, "Leader of the Pack" (1964).

The Ronettes, originally the Darling Sisters, were two sisters, Veronica (1943–2022) and Estelle Bennett (1941–2009), and their cousin, Nedra Talley (b 1946), from Washington Heights in New York. Their grandmother encouraged the tween and teens to harmonize. Legend has it that a wrong number or a tip from a teen magazine's editor introduced the group to music producer, Phil Spector (1939–2021), who was nicknamed the "First Tycoon of Teen" by Tom Wolfe in 1964. Phil put their images on the record sleeves, and their voices in his wall of sound (echo chambers, multi-tracking, and as many musicians as possible in the studio), a surround that suffocatingly resonated for lead singer, Ronnie Spector, when Phil married her and kept her prisoner in his mansion for seven years. But she escaped, an active representation of the era's feminist zeitgeist. Phil actually died as a prisoner after being found guilty of the 2003 murder of Lana Clarkson.

The Ronette's 1963 "Be My Baby" is the perfected synthesis of bubblegum, pop, and art rock.

During the Depression, the Brill Building, on 49th and Broadway in NYC, rented rooms to music-makers, and by the 1960s, generated hit songs for girl groups. In that skyrise with gold elevators, the songwriters, publishers, and musicians could negotiate deals and record their songs. Two of the Brill Building's songwriters, Carole King and Gerry Goffin, wrote "Will You Love Me Tomorrow." When The Shirelles sang it in 1961, the song became a hit.

The quartet—Doris Coley (1941–2000), Addie Harris (1940–82), Beverly Lee (b 1942), and Shirley Owens (b 1941)— met in high school, forming a group in 1957 that eventually became The Shirelles. When a teacher suggested they enter a music contest, the quartet wrote a song for it, 1958's "I Met Him on a Sunday," which attracted fans, including one fan's mother, who signed them to her label. With "Will You Love Me Tomorrow," The Shirelles became the first girl group to reach number one on the chart, attaining musical feminism with a song about a heart's vulnerability.

That a Black girl group reached number one can be interpreted as civil rights in music. Civil rights means that people of different skin colors have equal rights and equal access, and can mingle without threat. Historians mark 1954 as the beginning of the Civil Rights movement. The civil rights climate sang: in 1963, The Shirelles performed in the Salute to Freedom concert, a fundraiser for civil rights. The Dixie-Cups— the singing trio of sisters Barbara Ann and Rosa Lee Hawkins, and their cousin Joan Marie Johnson—topped the Beatles when their song, "Chapel of Love," reached number one in 1964.

Another example of civil rights in music is when married partners Berry and Raynoma Gordy established Hitsville, U.S.A., and created Motown. In 1959, Berry (b 1929) founded an independent record company, Motown, in Detroit, Michigan. Vocalist, music publisher, and music producer Raynoma (1937–2016) found the place to house the label. Located at 2648 West Grand Boulevard and nicknamed Hitsville U.S.A., the two-story house had a small studio, and furniture that felt like a disciplined home: functional, pretty, spare—space was organized for efficiency and order, with a piano in the middle of the upstairs living space where Berry lived. Among the many successful musicians and bands that came from Motown, a girl group reigned supreme on the charts: the Supremes were second only to the Beatles for hits in the 1960s.

Berry approached making hits from his experience working on an assembly line. He insisted on flawless physical appearance, practiced onstage moves, and perfected sounds. There was a room for each aspect of making records, from writing to recording to performing to promotion. Motown had quality control meetings, too. Berry called Motown's music the "sound of young America," encouraging the teen market. When songwriters such as Lamont Dozier, Brian Holland, and Eddie Holland achieved almost as much fame as Berry, and demanded more money for the songs they wrote, Berry decided to credit songwriters under the heading The Corporation, which is what Berry did when he signed the Jackson 5 in 1969.

Teen pop's sway can be heard with Motown's Stevie Wonder (b 1950). Instead of taking a bow after a show one night in 1962, twelve-year-old Stevie Wonder improvised a call and response with the audience. The audience loved it! "That particular night was an amazing night," Stevie said in the 2019 documentary, *Hitsville: The Making of Motown*. "The girls were screaming and all this kind of stuff. That was probably the, really, first time that I understood the power of, you know, when you do performance a certain way, you get the kind of reaction that you get. We blew the house *out*." With that improvisation, he came up with what became his first number one song in 1963—"Fingertips."

Female fans wield such power. In 1961, Freda Kelly left school at sixteen and joined a typing pool. She'd lived in Liverpool, England, for a few years, after migrating there from Ireland with her parents. One day, Freda went to a local club on her lunch hour. The Cavern was a cellar with arched walls and a stage, no ventilation, and backed up toilets. The first time she went, the Beatles were playing. She loved their leather and laughter and music. "I was hooked," she said. She loved the "razzmatazz" between the band and the audience, how the band engaged the audience, and she befriended them, hanging out with them at their lunchtime shows.

She was just seventeen when she replaced Roberta "Bobby" Brown as their official fan club secretary in 1962. She wrote the fan club newsletters, gathering information about the band members and their families, and writing it up, including pictures. Letters she'd pen for the newsletter seemed like an editor's note in a magazine—professional, and in the know, and in control. Freda answered the fan letters, and there were up to 2,000 letters a day! The Beatles gave a shout-out to Freda on one of their fan club Christmas recordings, and the shout-out begins the 2013 documentary about her, *Good Ol' Freda*.

By the time they got to America, the four-piece band included George Harrison (1943–2001) on guitar, John Lennon

(1940–80) on vocals and guitar, Paul McCartney (b 1942) on vocals and bass, and Ringo Starr (b 1940) on drums. They'd styled their hair in bowl cuts called moptops which gave them a playfully boyish look, and they wore matching suits, their pants tight and their shoes with heels. Their songs of love were catchy, hopeful, and sexy. 1962's "Please Please Me" is provocative, and the throb was in the excitement of the band's harmonizing and their melodies.

The Beatles arrived at New York's Kennedy Airport in America in February 1964. They were greeted by such astounding excitement that it was called Beatlemania. The four mop-topped white boys from England wore identical suits and shook their shaggy hair, generating innocent romance with their popular song, "I Want to Hold Your Hand." The band made hit after hit.

1964's *A Hard Day's Night*, a musical comedy about the band getting ready for a performance, garnered Oscar nominations. Its marketing of the band as a band with fans at the start of their career and when they arrived in America helped establish the band as astronomical pop stars. By 1965 they played at Shea Stadium to 57,000 people.

The erotic and romantic clamor around Elvis predicted Beatlemania. As Jonathan Gould says in Tom O'Dell's documentary, *How the Beatles Changed the World* (2017), "These girls were controlling public space. And nobody could do anything about it. It's a perfect example of what we would call bad behavior: screaming, yelling, weeping in public. This is bad behavior in one way or another. And yet, it was sanctioned. Not by the authorities, but by the Beatles themselves." The Beatles may have insulted their fans by calling them Apple Scruffs, but the band needed their fans. The musicians hid their girlfriends from the press, a star text to attract the fantasies of fans. The fans contribute an adoring energy (not to mention money) necessary for a musician's livelihood.

Groupies emerged in the 1960s on the cusp of Second Wave Feminism as the avant-garde of the sexual revolution, navigating old-fashioned double standards with daring independence. Fans with the band, groupies went further than just going to the shows. Lillian Roxon, author of 1969's *Rock Encyclopedia*, defined groupies as "fans who have dared to break the barriers between the audience and the performer." Art Blakey & the Jazz Messengers imply groupies in the title, "Backstage Sally," a 1963 composition by saxophonist, Wayne Shorter. Lillian said the word "groupie" surfaced in 1965–6 along with easy access to local bands.

Groupies were usually females because traditionally females were supposed to cheer males on but also because females were becoming sexually liberated. Groupies and SuperGroupies expressed the sexual liberation to come. SuperGroupies went on tour with the band, or became famous from their groupiedom, or had several intimate relationships with musicians. SuperGroupie Pamela Des Barres (b 1949) told me she "popped the pill on the Sunset Strip," referring to the birth control that had been approved in 1960. The pill, which females took, put all the health risks from potential side effects on females but gave females freedom from pregnancy and marriage, too.

Girls and women were shaping culture as they moved more freely through it. Musician and SuperGroupie, Cherry Vanilla, told me that fans and groupies called DJs and requested specific records; my mom remembered that she and her teen friends would make a song popular by requesting it; and Priscilla Presley (b 1945) said about her first meeting with Elvis, when she was fourteen and he was twenty-four, that the more she looked at him, the more he'd play music. *Star* magazine writer and editor, Don Berrigan, told me he created contests knowing that teen readers would enter them and boost record sales.

Beatles newsletter writer, Freda Kelly, said fans bought the 1962 Beatles song, "Love Me Do," even though many didn't even have a record player: "We bought it just to boost the sales," she said in *Good Ol' Freda*. The song sounds happy, with just a bit of melancholy—like the band is looking for love.

DJs ruled the airwaves, but so did fans, many of whom were female. Before the Beatles arrived in America, it was a teen girl fan who introduced one of their songs on American radio in 1963, chosen to do so because she'd written to request their music: fourteen-year-old Marsha Albert on DJ Carroll James's WWDC show with "I Want to Hold Your Hand."

Girl groups were popular, and so were songs by teen girls. Lesley Gore, whose producer was Quincy Jones, recorded "It's My Party" in 1963 at the age of sixteen. The song was a hit. The next year, on the *T.A.M.I. (Teen Age Music International) Show*, she sang "You Don't Own Me," a song written by two men, David White and John Madara. The hit song became the basis for an online women's voting campaign in 2017.

> You don't own me
> I'm not just one of your many toys

In the 1960s, when Lesley's songs were played on the radio and climbed the charts alongside the Beatles, fans reportedly camped out on her front lawn.

It could be argued that the Beatles, and the hard-rocking all-male bands of the '60s, replaced the popular, money-making, and chart-topping all-female bands and female-fronted songs in a patriarchal *coup d'etat* of sound. Groupies seemed to replace girl groups, a reinstatement of girls as cheerleaders rather than players, except with the GTOs, who became known as a groupie group. Patriarchy sexualizes females. And, because same-sex desire was criminalized and socially stigmatized, female groupies of girl groups were not made visible in the way female groupies of boy bands were. Also, many of the girl groups were engineered by males, their entrée to the world of music thereby more likely.

But the impact of seeing and hearing females as music-makers then was not diluted; reverberations in '70s teen pop can be found in Karen Carpenter, Cher, Marie Osmond, and Donna Summer. It's true that they achieved superstardom alongside men in the '70s, but their power predicts the increasing prevalence of females on the charts in future decades. And they each went (or were seen as) solo, most to great success. Girl groups also influenced countercultural values as well as '70s teen pop stars. For example, the harmonizing in the bite-sized songs of The Ramones, and the popular presence of girls and women and people of color onstage, on TV, on magazine covers, and on the radio.

Bubblegum pop was associated with girl groups. Girls made to seem confectionary in patriarchy were perfect for bubblegum. And it stuck. Its simple song structures, upbeat tempos, and catchy hooks made the music radio-friendly and teen/tween inviting. Bubblegum pop was also made by studio musicians, or by studio musicians with a teen pop idol singer. Catchy melodies with double entendres perfectly expressed the conundrum of pre-teen and teen sexuality: what the little girls and boys understand is something they don't actually comprehend. '70s teen pop emerged from the bubblegum pop of the 1960s and early 1970s.

The phrase itself has a grittily sweet basis: in New York, at a candy store in Washington Heights during the 1950s, aspiring songwriter Don Kirshner (1934–2011) met singer Robert Cassotto (1936–73), and they decided to work together. Soon after, they co-wrote their first published song, "Bubblegum Pop." But when Cassotto, under the stage name Bobby Darin, had a hit in 1958 with "Splish Splash," which he wrote on his own, they went separate ways. Don founded Aldon Music at the Brill Building, and nurtured talents such as Connie Francis and Neil Sedaka, making music geared toward a young audience.

Bubblegum pop was further fomented by television cartoons and cartoon bands, too. In 1966, Don was hired to work on the TV show, *The Monkees*, a band created by executives specifically for a TV show (which ran for two years), inspired by the success of the Beatles and their movie, *A Hard Day's Night*. Mickey Dolenz (b 1945), Davy Jones (1945–2012), Michael Nesmith (1942–2021), and Peter Tork (1942–2019) were hired after auditioning. Released in 1966, "Last Train to Clarksville" and "I'm a Believer" were smash hits but the alliance was not; the band members sang but didn't play instruments; the session musicians were not credited; the second album was released without the band's knowledge. But by their third album, Don was gone and the band played their own instruments. The Monkees, a band who at first didn't exist except in a storyline about a band who wanted to exist, believed in their right to autonomy and creative expression.

Don reportedly said he wanted to work with a band that didn't talk back, so he created The Archies, a cartoon pop band for an animated TV show of the same name, which ran for one year in 1968. The Archies played bubblegum pop by session musicians hired by Don for the TV series, a series based on a comic book that began in 1941. The all-white band included two women, Betty Cooper and Veronica Lodge. The best-selling song of 1969 was theirs: "Sugar, Sugar," one of whose writers was Andy Kim, who worked in the Brill Building. The Ohio Express released "Yummy Yummy Yummy" and "Chewy Chewy" at the end of the '60s, too (in 1968), songs that sounded just as bubblegum—fun and unburdened by complexity, a counter to the counterculture.

The uniformity of girl groups and boy bands—evidenced by the matching stage outfits they wore and their harmonizing—could seem conformist. But fun-loving unification can move complicated social changes forward. Being gay was a criminal offense until 1980. But the Mafia-owned Stonewall Inn on Christopher Street in NYC was a gathering spot for mostly boys and men but sometimes girls and women, most of whom were gay. Same-sex couples could mingle and dance together, make-out, and dress as the opposite sex. In 1969, the Stonewall Inn became a site of resistance to police entrapment and police brutality. The Stonewall Rebellion lasted six days and five nights as club-goers vamped and threw coins and chanted in chorus lines and tagged the walls with graffiti that proclaimed "Gay Power" while police arrested several people, throwing them in a paddy wagon. Tear gas and nightsticks flew. After the rebellion ended, people went back to the trashed bar and danced to the music.

The Stonewall Inn jukebox was wonderful—songs sung by people of different colors, genders, and ages. Selections included songs by teen pop idols such as the Beatles, Elvis, Frank Sinatra, and Stevie Wonder mixed in with Shirley Bassey, Judy Garland, Ronnie Spector and the Ronettes, and Barbra Streisand. The song on the jukebox that represented the 1960s as it rocketed into the '70s—"Aquarius/Let the Sunshine In"—was there in the jukebox, too. The 5th Dimension played it live in 1969 at the Harlem Cultural Festival. The band wasn't invited to play the more widely publicized Woodstock that same year—but the massive Woodstock audience knew all the words to the song and spontaneously sang it, said Danyel Smith at the *Popular Music Books in Process* series.

Counterculture

In 1962's Cuban Missile Crisis, the United States and the Soviet Union did not set off their atomic bombs, avoiding war. Atomic bombs would kill everyone, no matter what side they're (we're) on. Accordingly, the counterculture of the 1960s demanded progressive change, and music was going there.

In 1969, Newport Festival organizer George Wein added funk and rock to his usually all-jazz event when Sly and the Family Stone and Led Zeppelin took the stage. George said all four days were sold out, and they attracted 80,000 people (the festival usually attracted 35,000–50,000). By the mid-'70s, jazz and swing, which had once provided the bulk of the profits in the music industry, provided less than 3 percent.

During the 1960s, in America, there was a newly profound doubting of adults and government. The lynching of Blacks; the Nazi persecution of Jewish people, gay people, people with physical "disabilities," people with mental "illness," and artists; the forced confinement of Japanese people; and the Red Scare (which cornered, questioned, and punished people for their political beliefs) contributed to a questioning of authority in America. The controlled hairstyles (slicked back or short for men, curled and set with every hair in place for women) and the girdled bodies of both got loose as many people challenged the status quo.

The counterculture opposed or challenged social norms. The counterculture in America, which developed during the mid-1960s and lasted until the mid-'70s, sought an alternative to established social mores, expressing a do-it-yourself, or DIY, communal spirit in the food cooperatives, communes, open marriages, and underground newspapers and zines they created. Drug experimentation—earlier heralded by the 1950s Beat poets—included hallucinogenic drugs, which expanded consciousness and physical sensation. People burned draft cards (draft cards enforced military service and combat) and bras. The Civil Rights and Sexual Liberation movements along with protests against the Vietnam War, the development of the birth control pill for women, and riots in the streets demonstrated that many people did not want what was prescribed; rather, the people wanted peace, freedom, choice, and equality. Also, individuality—men grew their hair long and shed their ties, and women took off their girdles and went braless. Clothes with wild colorful prints, stripes, and tie-dye were popular. Skirts got short and jeans flared at the feet. In 1969, Woodstock (three days), the Harlem Cultural Festival (six weeks), and Altamont (one night) were large-scale concerts that signaled the height and the end of the 1960s, but not the end of the counterculture. They also signaled the importance of the musician.

Ava Gardner, the movie star Artie Shaw had asked to sing in his band, danced with Duke Ellington at the Waldorf-Astoria in Manhattan, and a photo of the two dancing together was published in the May 1969 issue of *Jet* magazine in a key change: a mixed-race couple on the dance floor pictured happily in the media.

Because of technology, information (and music) was more readily available: television showed footage of what it actually looked like to be on the front lines in the war, in the midst of civil unrest, and in the middle of violent protests. Assassinations and murders were made more visible: President John F. Kennedy in 1963; human rights activist Malcolm X in 1965; Civil Rights leader Dr. Martin Luther King Jr. in 1968; and US Senator Robert F. Kennedy in 1968. Hate crimes were made more obvious to more people; for example, those done by the Ku Klux Klan, a group of racist white terrorists who formed after the Civil War. The KKK killed adolescents Addie May Collins, Carol Denise McNair, Cynthia Wesley, and Carole Rosamond Robertson on a Sunday in 1963 when they went to a Baptist church; Medger Evers in his front yard in 1963 (he was a field officer of the NAACP, the National Association for the Advancement of Colored People, a diverse group begun in 1909); and James Chaney, Michael Schwerner, and Andrew Goodman in 1964 (they were members of CORE, the Congress of Racial Equality, begun in 1942).

But the Voting Rights Act of 1965 ensured that (more) Black people could vote. The draft ended in 1973. An American president resigned in 1974 after audio recordings of his racist comments provided proof that he had lied to the American people. The Vietnam War, which began in 1955, ended in 1975. Rock 'n roll, energetic and happy, was a counterpart to the suffering. There was a sweetness somewhere. Wasn't there?

Play

What makes a song popular? My youthful understanding was that a popular song was an organic creation of music by friends who were irresistibly compelled to play music. Their talent was natural, easily and immediately expressed, the music they made inherently worthy of recognition, their radio airplay and eventual fame, fortune, and recognition inevitable. It turns out there is a lot more strategy, ambition, and practice involved than I ever imagined. It also turns out that socialization tries to limit, inhibit, repress, and punish diversity and variety, reinforcing a binary of listening and creating, rewarding only a very specific manner of physical and aural expression. But we keep trying to play.

What is a pop song? An abbreviation of the word "popular" combined with "song" which can be understood as songs that climb the charts. Charts are rankings based on radio airplay and sales. Airplay originally included radio and jukeboxes and currently includes digital streaming. Purchase of vinyl records, cassette tapes, CDs, downloads, and streaming reflect sales. Payola and marketing affect sales as well as disc jockey preferences, charismatic or corporate influence, and audience demand. Music journalist Danyel Smith told me, "Pop is the people's choice." And although pop charts and award systems are deeply flawed, they are what we have, and they are more accurate since 1991's SoundScan, which tracks sales through registered barcodes.

The pop song itself is tidy, neat, and self-contained; even with the potential wildness of a guitar, drum, or wail, the expression is kept under control and usually under three to five minutes. Typically the lyrics are clear, but sometimes sounds are uncontained by words, and the repetition of words and sound encourages listeners to sing or hum along. It could be considered manipulative if one listens too closely: the song's "hook" grabs listeners.

At the very great risk of ruining the music for me as well as for you, I will not deep dive into this in the hopes that I can retain some mystery and magic in the song for us all, so here is the general structure of a typical pop song: a verse, a chorus, a verse, a chorus, a bridge, and then a chorus. The hook is the melody, and chord progressions build interest. Lyrics with a story can change with different verses that offer a similar melody. The bridge does something new amidst the repetition to keep listeners interested, and to keep listeners craving the suddenly missing repetition that then returns.

Choruses and hooks reinforce harmony and melody. The standard pop song is usually about three minutes long because of how many grooves could be stored on the record before the sound quality suffered on 78s, the early albums. Also, shorter songs on the radio meant more room for advertisers on the radio program, who paid for radio air space. Technology and capitalism informed the length of the song. But longer songs found airplay, too; long songs and mixing them meant more time for dancing.

What is teen pop? The music of teen pop during the '70s could be defined by music marketed to teens and tweens (teens are 13–19 years old, tweens are 9–12), with prevalence determined by coverage in teen magazines, radio airplay, album and cassette sales, merchandising (the presence and sale of objects that represent the musician or band), TV or film appearances, and whether or not the album went gold, platinum, or diamond.

But that bothers me because it gives all the power to business people, DJs, and ambitious music-makers, ignoring the many musical loves of tweens and teens, as though they are only manipulable consumers. Is it teen pop only if it's marketed to tweens and teens? If so, then that ignores the power of the tweens and teens (often females) who drive sales, and puts too much power to corporate-think tanks, a capitalist individual, or entrepreneurs. Besides, teen pop goes hand in hand with the fans. They like music adults like, too. They listen to the music their parents and parents' friends play. They buy music marketed to them and music that isn't marketed to them. And what about independent fan clubs? Fan clubs create their own endorsements. Teen pop is heart-shaped.

Teen pop includes teen-aged singers but also adult singers; songs marketed to tweens and teens as well as some marketed to adults; and teen idols, a few of whom are primarily movie stars rather than musical artists. Teen idols are featured in magazines marketed to teens and tweens. In previous decades, teen pop was marketed as heterosexual and to teen and tween girls, but in the '70s, gender-bending and a male fan base was recognized. I think teen pop is any pop song with a tween or teen fan base.

1970–3

American Top 40, a syndicated radio program, launched in 1970. It played songs based on the *Billboard Hot 100*, which ranked popularity by airplay and sales. The show aired on seven different radio stations, and by the early 1980s it played globally on five hundred stations and on the Armed Forces Radio Network. Casey Kasem hosted *AT40* until 1988, providing biographical information on the songs and reading

Play

aloud dedications sent in by listeners. I remember his clear and warm voice in between songs during the three-hour weekly program. Maybe his voice reminded me of the character Casey played, Shaggy, on the popular animated TV show about teen-aged detectives, *Scooby-Doo*, that I watched regularly, a character who became vegetarian at vegan Casey's insistence. Did the countdown launch '70s teen pop?

Or maybe it was a cartoon based on a comic book. Josie and the Pussycats starred in an animated TV series named after them from 1970 to 1971. The storyline about an all-female rock band was published by Archie Comics as a comic book series from 1963 to 1982. Josie and the Pussycats are a trio of women who write and perform their own music. The storyline shows them rehearsing, carrying their own equipment, and booking and playing gigs. The sexploitation film formula of featuring three females—one Black, one white blonde, and one white brunette—nevertheless sent a feminist message: Females could be in their own band. Artist Dan DeCarlo created the storyline inspired by wife, Josie, and her cat costume. *Josie and the Pussycats* gave their mostly female readership the idea that they could do what boys and men do: be in a band, self-promote, and explore the world by going out into it.

Or maybe it was *The Brady Bunch*, which ran from 1969 to 1974, then went into syndication. An American comedy show with half-hour episodes airing weekly on TV, it told the story of a family and their housekeeper, and every episode would focus on one of the characters. The parents, Carol and Mike Brady, each had three kids from previous marriages, marriages that ended when their spouses died. Carol's kids were Marcia, Jan, and Cindy. Mike's kids were Greg, Peter, and Bobby. The kids ranged in age from 6 to 13, and by the series' end, the oldest was eighteen—pre-teen and teen pop in formation. Most of the episodes featured storylines about pre-teen and teen issues represented by one or some of the children, although a few episodes included adult concerns. The live-in housekeeper, Alice, was like a member of the family, with significant air time and storylines about her life, too.

The theme song's lyrics were written by series creator, Sherwood Schwartz, and the music credited to Frank De Vol, who had arranged music for swing artists such as Ella Fitzgerald and Nat King Cole. The Peppermint Trolley Company were the pilot's studio musicians, and possible contributors to the lyrics, chords, and arrangement of the theme song. For the first season, more session musicians did the vocals. By 1970, with the success of *The Partridge Family*, a competing show about a family in a band who actually sang on the show and released albums as The Partridge Family, *The Brady Bunch* theme song was sung by the actors who played the kids in the show. After that, the TV family released albums on which the kids sang as a band called The Brady Bunch Kids (with session musicians). "It's a Sunshine Day" was performed by the Brady Kids in the episode, "Amateur Nite" (Season 4, Episode Sixteen, January 26, 1973). As they sing, they look American wholesome in their vivid colors, clean clothes and tidy hair, synchronized dance moves, and good cheer.

The series is significant in how it reflects the absorption of countercultural ideas in mainstream culture. The episode, "Getting Davy Jones" (Season 3, Episode Twelve, December 10, 1971), proclaims female agency. As president of the local Davy Jones Fan Club, Marcia promised her high school friends that Davy from The Monkees (another band born from a TV show) would sing in person at the high school prom. She tried various resourceful ways to ask him—she went to the Royal Towers Hotel where he was staying; she called the hotel; she composed a telegram; she dressed as a boy and pretended to be a busser at the hotel; she showed up at a TV show where he was a guest; and she showed up at his recording session, where we viewers were treated to his singing "Girl." Her parents and Alice and Sam called in favors to no avail. Alice commiserated; remembering that she wore black bobbysox for a month when she heard that Frank Sinatra was married.

But Marcia had said, "If I say I'll get him, I'll get him." And she did! Davy could overhear her on the studio mic as she explained her conundrum to his manager. Then the popular singer unexpectedly showed up at her cool house and gave her an album! As they made plans to go together to the prom, she kissed him on the cheek, and he said, "How about the flipside?" So she kissed him again on the other side of his face! The Brady Kids launched as a musical group after that.

It's important to recognize that resourceful Marcia was thinking with goal-oriented logic, similar to fans named groupies in the '60s. Second Wave Feminism from the '60s and during the '70s sought an agency that didn't (have to) rely on sexuality. But also in the '70s, sexual liberation meant women could choose their erotic partners, have more than one partner, say no to unwanted attention, and refuse marriage. And as of 1973, abortions became safe and legal with *Roe* v. *Wade*. Girls and women could decide what to do with their own bodies.

In early 1973, in the *Roe* v. *Wade* case, America determined that the government did not have a right to unduly determine whether or not a female can have a safe and legal abortion. Her right to privacy was constitutional and therefore included the right to decide what to do with the pregnancy of her own body. Abortions were made legal. There were restrictions, and more were made over the years since, especially affecting girls and women of color, and those with few financial or health insurance resources. In 2022, the right to a safe and legal abortion—and privacy about it—was taken away from females. Individual states could decide if abortions were legal.

When I wrote about *Roe* v. *Wade* in terms of Marcia Brady and the "Getting Davy Jones" episode, *Roe* v. *Wade* was in its last few days of national legality. It was overturned on June 24, 2022, today as I write this. The lyrics to the song Davy sang on the show compliment the girl in the title as it places the entire responsibility of his response to her on her.

> Girl
> Look what you've done to me

Patriarchy putting the entirety of sexuality's responsibility on females: from inspiring desire to the costs of sexuality and pregnancy; the birth control and its side effects; and the raising of children. Females are judged with punition for how they handle what should be a shared responsibility and a private decision.

♥ ♥ ♥

When does sexual agency require adult boundaries? It's also important to consider the ages of Marcia and Davy: Maureen McCormick was fifteen, playing a high schooler, and Davy was twenty-five, playing himself, a professional musician. The on-screen kiss was chaste and sweet. But the reality is also in the early years of the '70s some groupies were nicknamed "baby groupies" because they were underage. The cultural encouragement of sexual exploration alongside the increasingly elevated status of musicians motivated underage fans to be intimate with musicians.

Bobby Sherman's 1971 hit song, "Waiting at the Bus Stop," sounds exciting and vaguely disturbing: the singing narrator—who is old enough to drive—circles the block several times, winking at a "little girl" waiting at the bus stop, a "sweet young thing" he wants to meet and take to the picture show. He admits how lonely he is, and the music sounds groovy, like the bright colors on his album covers. It's a toe-tapping patriarchal codependence and creepiness that targets tween and teen girls. But Bobby really does seem lovely. I only choose his song because it's such an excellent example of the way language lives, with all its complications. A mature-looking teen pop star, Bobby Sherman (b 1943), was a hitmaker and TV star fans adored, who segued from the '60s to the '70s with his grown-up man voice, collar-length hair with the side part, a friendly smile, and chipper instrumentation. When teen magazine, *Tiger Beat*, ran "Bobby Sherman's Dream Girl Contest," the magazine received two million entries. Two million! Girls were dreaming.

On the West Coast in the early '70s, underage girls flocked to the Sunset Strip, looking for fun and freedom in the skin-loving sunshine and exciting nightlife of a musically happening Los Angeles. In their platform shoes, glittery halter tops, and satin short-shorts, baby groupies frequented rock clubs and hotel coffee shops, kicked their competition on the dance floor, fed frenemies razor-blade sandwiches, and cavorted with musicians who attained rock star status. In all, they established a new kind of cultural mythology based on fact.

Led Zeppelin's self-proclaimed golden god singer, Robert Plant (b 1948), and the band's allegedly devil-worshiping guitarist, Jimmy Page (b 1944), wrote about the cherry lips and queenly brows of their dreaming teen-aged fans in a dubious tribute with Led Zeppelin's 1975 song, "Sick Again."

> Clutching pages from your teenage dream …
> How fast you learn the downhill slide

They've been nicknamed baby groupies in the press, but the song calls the underage fans L.A. Queens. When asked what it was like to be on the scene and an L.A. Queen, Morgana Welch (b 1956) told me, "It was magical, like being on drugs … We just enveloped in this world, it was their world, but you were part of it." Music journalist, Ann Powers, observes, "As has happened so many times within the realm of popular music, exploitation and the feeling of freedom merge in the troubling, celebrated figure of the teenage queen."

♥ ♥ ♥

Teen pop, with its veneer of cheer and innocence, often hid what the musicians truly felt or experienced: sex and drugs and lots of money. Singing songs steeped in a culture's suffering and evolving, language evolves as attitudes evolve. Some teen pop artists experienced being ripped off and raped, then replaced, as happened with the bands Menudo and the Bay City Rollers. But some of the music hinted at or suggested sublime or wonderful experience, as with The Partridge Family's "I Think I Love You" (1970) in which singer David Cassidy's voice obediently follows the almost hurried pace of the song, but here and there the intonation of his true voice: passionate and ambitious, mature with need, and working hard to attain a goal.

The Partridge Family was a TV show about a garage band that aired from 1970 to 1974. Based on a real-life band, The Cowsills, the American musical sitcom was about a family of six musicians led by their widowed mom who lived and toured together. Television's ability to nurture a musician's popularity proved instrumental.

The Partridge Family's 1970 hit single, "I Think I Love You," transformed adult male crooning into teenage dreams and its fictional teen star into a bona fide teen pop idol; David Cassidy's voice sounded like a young man's, not an adult's, vocalizing the 1960s countercultural tenet of never trusting anyone over

Play

thirty. He was twenty years old playing the role of a teen when he joined the TV show. In 1970, his long hair and happening clothes conveyed a reassurance; he was simultaneously old enough and young enough to be cool (he wore a necklace!), his voice soft enough for youth but deep enough for potential command. Gentle! Hard! Wow! David's collar-length hair and puka shell necklace signaled female signifiers, attracting female fans.

And the music was fun. When Elvis's daughter, Lisa Marie, was just a few years old in the early '70s, she loved the show and sang along to "I Think I Love You." Her mom, Priscilla, recorded her and sent the recordings to a touring Elvis. Those recordings can be heard in the opening and closing of "Raven," a song Lisa Marie released as an adult in 2005.

The naiveté of countercultural idealism (and the hope before reality sobers) is personified in David Cassidy. The son of show business professionals, actors Evelyn Ward and Jack Cassidy, David was born in 1950 New York and raised in New Jersey, sometimes by his grandparents. David's first professional performance was in a musical on Broadway, in 1969's *The Fig Leaves Are Falling*. David moved to LA and acted in several TV shows.

Jack was a Broadway matinee star, and David's stepmother, Shirley Jones, an Academy-Award-winning actor. Shirley played his mom on the hit show, and was the only other cast member besides David to sing on the Partridge albums. Shirley had longtime acting credibility and was earning a living playing the part of a widowed woman who earned a living doing something cool as she raised a family. Her story, and the show's story, is countercultural: it's a message about women's talents and competence and power beyond and including family.

Their teen pop tour bus began the imagery and the theme song for the show; its playful design a reference to the De Stijl art style of bold shapes and bright colors—Modernism's gleeful and scary freedom along with its godless subjectivity setting the stage for the idolization of the pop star.

1971's "I Woke Up in Love This Morning" from the Partridge album, *Sound Magazine*, achieved the perfect blend of teen pop romance with a subtly sophisticated implication: what happened the night before? The title of the album suggests the popularity of music magazines. Former teen idol, Paul Anka, co-wrote with Wes Farrell the song, "One Night Stand," for the album, a double entendre of a one-night music gig and a one-night sexual experience:

> A pretty face, another place I never get to know
> a one night stand, another show

He felt pressure to perform! Oh he was sad and alone! He could be rescued! The happy humming chorus keeping the heavy meaning light enough to sing along to.

Merch for *The Partridge Family* included purses, vinyl, lockets, t-shirts, towels, dolls, buses, thermoses, radios, bubblegum cards, cereal boxes, comic books, pillowcases, and clocks. A plastic guitar! A lunchbox is in the Smithsonian.

David resented not cashing in on the merch, so he toured on the weekends. His first show sold out in one day. He also resented *The Partridge Family*; David didn't want to be a teen pop idol, and he wasn't Keith. But he was contractually obligated, as well as pressured by family. And then he renegotiated his contract with the show after realizing he'd signed when he was a minor. Clever self-care! But according to his memoir, he didn't receive the money from his merch.

In 1972, *Rolling Stone* magazine featured David naked on its cover with an accompanying story titled "David Cassidy: Naked

Lunch Box" by Robin Green. The word "box" is slang for vulva, and "naked lunch" refers to a sometimes banned series of vignettes written by William Burroughs (which were published in 1959; the issue includes an interview with wife-killing William). This play with language is a hallmark of teen pop, and of '70s gender-blending.

The cover, shot by Annie Leibovitz (b 1949), showed David nude on a bed of grass, arms raised. He was twenty-two years old and tired of the career that he didn't want in the first place. He felt like a puppet to his image, and the magazine cover challenged that image. He thanked Annie for the photo.

David told *Behind the Music* that he wanted to play like Jimi Hendrix (1942–70) and not like Keith Partridge: "Inside was this raging teen-ager who wanted to say *this* is who I am," he said, making powerful vocal sounds as he played air guitar to demonstrate. But he was nominated for an Emmy and had earned millions! By age twenty-one, he earned more than any performer on the globe, and had a bigger fan club than the Beatles and Elvis! His dressing room had a couch and lots of mirrors! Trapped in pretty boy whiteness, the massive amounts of sex with adoring fans didn't seem to help. Many fans fell in love with Keith—not David—a character who wore bunny suits and cowboy outfits on the show. Like when Elvis had to sing to a dog on a TV show, the teen pop idol felt demeaned. His attire at his own concerts seemed like a circus performer, with sparkling top hat, a jacket with tails, and a cane.

"The teen girl attraction to Cassidy wasn't just about of lust; it was also about identification. Much like the girls who adored him, Cassidy was an object to fetishize, but he was never allowed to take control of his own life," writes Kate H., in "David Cassidy: A Brief and Belated Eulogy."

David was more popular than the Beatles—and there was only one of him.

During the Second World War, when swing and bobbysoxers pronounced teen-agers as culturally impactful, Americans began to wonder why young men who weren't legally old enough to vote in their country were being drafted to fight (and die) for their country. In 1971, the year after *The Partridge Family* debuted, the voting age was lowered from twenty-one to eighteen when the 26th Amendment was approved. The singular power of a singing teen idol and swinging tweens and teens showcase the political sway of a youthquake.

♥ ♥ ♥

When Michael Jackson was a kid in Gary, Indiana, being raised as a Jehovah's Witness by parents, Katherine and Joe, he befriended one of the mice in his kitchen. Joe killed the mouse and broke Michael's heart. At least, that's how the story goes in the 1992 miniseries, *The Jacksons: An American Dream*.

When Michael was fourteen, he sang a song about friendship in his 1972 song, "Ben." The song about friendship was written for a movie about a rat, and it was Michael's first number one single as a solo act. An outcast who loved animals, I thought a song about a friendship with a rat meant the singer was sensitive and kind, seeing beauty where others saw ugliness and were afraid. The song itself moved listeners into the cradle of its mood, its smooth chorus an adult syrup, off-putting and endurable.

Around that time, I regularly watched *The Jackson 5ive*, an animated half-hour TV show that ran from 1971 to 1973, syndicated in the 1980s. The show was based on the real-life family in a band, a band that began in the early 1960s. Michael seemed like my friend.

And Randy Jackson seemed like a future husband to fan Karen Rolfe, who for a Catholic school assignment about marriage enacted her pretend wedding to him—a traditional Italian wedding that had lots of champagne and cannoli. "The dancing was everything," she told me about her love for the band.

The music on the show was played by studio musicians, the band's voices were spoken by actors, and the show's producer, Robert Balser, directed colorful animation similar to his work on 1968's animated film, *The Beatles: Yellow Submarine*: psychedelic, with gestural lines and popping color. Each boy's face in a heart on *The Jackson 5ive* promoted the idea of the band as heartthrobs and teen pop idols. Indeed, the opening image of the first episode is of an adoring audience in the balcony. The boys' bodies dance with friendly abandon and repetition, their flowing clothes groovy and contemporary, in bright colors such as orange, fuchsia, and green. They were on the side of youth with their adventures, pet rodents, and playfulness.

The five bandmates were brothers: Jackie (b 1951), Tito (b 1953), Jermaine (b 1954), and Marlon (b 1957, whose twin brother, Brandon, died at birth). Michael, born in 1958, was the youngest in the band, but not the family—Randy was born in 1961, and Janet in 1966. Two more sisters include Rebbie, born in 1950, and La Toya, born in 1956. JohVonnie was born in 1974 when Joe had an affair with Cheryle Terrell.

Joe was strict and reportedly abused the children. His discipline included music practice; the kids spent their childhoods rehearsing. They won several talent contests including a talent show at the Apollo. The band's name was inspired by Evelyn Leahy, the organizer of the fashion show where the band made their first appearance, in 1965.

And although Motown's Berry Gordy was not interested in the demo Joe sent him in 1965, by 1968 Berry invited them back.

The happy jaunt of the Jackson 5ive's "I Want You Back" (1969) combines a sensational beat with a youthful voice in the lead. While the deeper voiced chorus of his older brothers sounds mature, Michael Jackson's singing sounds young—the voice of youth's confidence and belief in itself, asserting itself. It felt like the kind of recognition kids want: that they matter, and that their feelings are real. The song went to number one on the pop charts. Age ranges in the band expanded the audience. And when Randy made an appearance on drums, the band furthered its youthful charm.

"ABC" (1970) sounds like the plaid they wore: multilayered, with brightness and repetition throughout, creating a complexity that sounds simple. A youthful voice telling a girl to "shake it" while the alphabet's opening trifecta is recited and sung feels less like a sexual threat and more like a playful command. The Jackson 5ive posed topless on teen magazines such as *Right On!*, complicating the youthful awareness of sexual physicality with adult profit-making motives.

Lucie Vaughn, a devoted '70s teen pop fan and my friend from high school, remembered a portable record player that she toted from room to room when she was five years old. The two albums she always toted? "The Jackson 5ive's *Third Album*, and *The Donny Osmond Album*. It had to be the whole album," she told me, she didn't just want to hear one song, and those two albums were perfect. She loved that their voices sounded like little girls. Michael Jackson and Donny Osmond joked about how their pop songs were about a rat and a dog— topics that appealed to teen and tween kiddos, too.

Lucie kept loving them as she became a tween, and told me why they were so important to her: the music made her happy.

The music makes her happy today! And she first heard it in the "pre-dating era of a young girl's life," when magic was possible, which makes the music even more precious. "They're going to sweep you away, or they're going to sing you somewhere," she told me.

Lucie remembered desegregated busing. Although 1954's *Brown* v. *Board of Education* sought integration through busing kids of many colors to school, during the '70s segregation continued. Lucie remembered the violence around it in her hometown of Louisville, KY, and remembered being bused to a predominantly Black school. But it wasn't violent for her; everyone welcomed her. The Jackson 5ive had introduced her, a white kid watching a show about Black kids, to a world that came true when she was bussed; integration was happening.

From 1976 to 1977, the family had their own variety show, *The Jacksons*. The youngest of the ten siblings, Janet, would also guest on a popular TV show from 1977 to 1979, *Good Times*, and, during the 1980s, become a major pop star with her solo singing career.

The '70s ended the way the decade began: with Michael Jackson as a teen pop star. Michael's 1979 *Off the Wall* was a success. And unlike so many teen pop stars, Michael was on his way to superstardom. Writer Shana L. Redmond wrote to me: "Jackson made something spectacular—in sound and the dancing body—from something very humble."

During the '70s, stadium-sized venues and sprawling festivals replaced intimate clubs for shows: the band was further away from most of the audience, and the audience was so vast it seemed like a political rally. Fans lit lighters and held them aloft in allegiance to the song. The song—and the band, and the band's management—could now make even more money. As could shows about music.

Soul Train was on every Saturday when I was in second grade. I watched it repeatedly. So did sonic legend Aretha Franklin's kids, which is why she asked if she could perform on the show. That's when the show's creator and host, Don Cornelius (1936–2012), knew he had a hit series.

The hour-long variety show first aired in 1970 Chicago, and it was broadcast nationally from 1971 to 2006. *Soul Train* showcased music: dancers dancing to it, musicians lip-syncing to it, and Don introducing it all. His slow baritone made me pay attention, a cool contrast to the wild dancing all around him. The best was when the dancers danced like this: they formed two rows across from each other, with space in the middle for people to dance down, the rows on either side constantly moving forward as dancers moved from the top of the row and danced together down the middle. Everyone got a turn. There was also a scramble board, and while the music played and dancers danced, two people unscrambled letters on a board to answer a question such as the name of a sports star or writer. When they were done, they danced. *Soul Train* was spelling it out.

Neon flashed and multicolored disco lights glowed, the art deco design of the dance space curved and brightened for a '70s friendliness. Elevated platforms above the crowd on the dance floor featured a few more dancers. The clothes! Everyone had on different styles and wow! What styles!

Don, who hosted the show until 1993, was a radio announcer who conceptualized, produced, and owned the show, the only Black-owned show on TV. It was like being in a brightly lit club. Musical guests were numerous, and included legends. Christopher P. Lehman told National Public Radio that when The Jackson 5ive appeared on the show in 1973, Michael did a robot dance he'd learned from watching *Soul Train* dancers.

Play

The show's theme song was not its first theme song, but it was the first theme song of a TV show to make the charts, and it was sung by a group that began ten years earlier, when the vocalists were in high school. Mostly an instrumental, and written by Kenny Gamble and Leon Huff after Don Cornelius approached them in 1973 to write the theme, "T.S.O.P. (The Sound of Philadelphia)" featured the racially mixed studio band, MFSB (Mother Father Sister Brother), with vocals sung by The Three Degrees, whose members were a revolving trio but at the time of the theme song's recording were Sheila Ferguson (b 1947), Valerie Holiday (b 1947), and founding member Fayette Pinkney (1948–2009). The Three Degrees formed in 1963, when Fayette, Shirley Porter, and Linda Turner were teens in high school. "T.S.O.P. (The Sound of Philadelphia)" was so popular it was released as a single, and went gold in 1974. The Three Degrees, with their glamorous and sparkling gowns, their beautifully graceful and synchronized choreography, and their disciplined harmony veering from light like light to gospel-inflection like faith, created a sound that can be sourced as the origin of disco as well as the sound of a city.

The train in the show's animation looked like it was dancing, rolling along the tracks in a funky groove with a chanted refrain, making sparks on the tracks and smoke and fire as the soul train traveled over the globe and through the city, amidst mountains and tall buildings, with billboards for Ultra Sheen and Afro Sheen. The bright gold lettering of the show's name seemed to gleam.

♥ ♥ ♥

Earth Day began in 1970, a countercultural interest in global health. In contrast, inflation, rising housing costs, and rising unemployment meant that it cost more to live. American dependence on oil kept growing, as did the damage that dependence does to the economy, human bodies, animals, and the planet. The OPEC embargo in 1973 created a gas shortage, an example of how contrary motives and competing interests can maintain peace or create war as various countries negotiate their exchange of resources and/or military weapons. Many Americans were in love with listening to the radio as they drove—and the cars they drove ran on oil.

In America, where individual states have historically determined the legal driving age in that state, some drivers could be as young as fourteen, but teens could usually get a license to drive by age sixteen. At first, "horseless carriages" did not require a license or an exam, but slowly each state required them, and by 1959, a driver's license and a written exam were required in every state to legally drive. Wielding a machine that weighs on average 4,000 pounds and has always polluted the environment is a huge responsibility. Top down or windows open, the radio playing, wind in your hair and on your skin, the delights of driving deny the severe pain driving can cause. The teen-aged brain won't fully develop until adulthood, which means that the reality of consequences is understood as a concept but not as an actuality. Teen tragedy tunes, such as KISS's "Detroit Rock City" (1976), however, point to a growing awareness.

Interestingly, a driver's license serves as a proof of identification. Which I think signifies the teen's growing importance in culture. And by the '70s, cars gave teens a place to be alone, without their parents or a chaperone.

A song about a car written by Warren Casey and Jim Jacobs, "Greased Lightnin," with its vaguely suggestive title and its reference to the car being a "pussy wagon," point to the objectification of the female body. A song written for a play in 1971 but further popularized in the 1978 musical movie *Grease*—which is about teen-agers in the 1950s—the song makes it clear that young men are driving the car, and that cars can be a place to have sex. Indeed, one of the film's starring characters worries that she's pregnant; back seat trysts are alluded to, and the film's ending takes place in a car.

Grease's star and singer, John Travolta (b 1954), became a teen idol who graced the cover of many a teen magazine in the '70s, co-starring in *Welcome Back, Kotter*, a TV sitcom from 1975 to 1979 about high school, and starring in another massively successively box-office musical—1977's *Saturday Night Fever*, a movie about a nineteen year old who lives with his parents, works at a paint store, and dazzles on the disco dance floor.

With songs that encourage dancing as well as romantic and sexual activity—and sometimes violence—teen pregnancy must be addressed in music. And yet, songs rarely discuss how to safely avoid unwanted pregnancy or unwanted sex.

Rape in the back of a car was re-edited in *Saturday Night Fever* to make it look less horrifying (it was horrifying anyway). An attempted rape was normalized. A tragedy befalls another character, too, when he commits suicide because of a girlfriend's unwanted pregnancy. Lyrics that model non-rapist behavior would be wonderful. Access to safe and legal abortions as well as education about birth control are also rarely mentioned in songs, and that's a lack not just in teen pop songs. I long for the time when lyrics in every genre cover more territory than poetic abstractions and clever or lovely reference to human emotions.

A popular song by Cher tried to address more than romance, discussing racism in 1973's "Half-Breed," written by Mary Dean and Al Capps. She's been criticized for singing the song that was written for her because the title of the song is derogatory and because she isn't Native American.

Backed by the little known but highly sought Wrecking Crew in the song, Cher in feathers and casually astride a horse sang about being insulted for her skin color and mixed race. Cher's crooked teeth presented a new beauty, her contralto voice venturing forth unembarrassed and strong and in narrative control, and the music bright, jangly, and emphatic. Her walk a casual strut on the television show that included her name.

The *Sonny & Cher Comedy Hour* (1971–4), with its blend of singing, comedy skits, guest stars, and animation, featured the hosts, Sonny and Cher, a married couple, whose hit song from 1967, "The Beat Goes On," blended in with the show's opening theme song, their bodies sketched in the opening graphics, and their faces repeated over and over on the lit circles that served as the stage backdrop to their lively shtick.

"The Beat Goes On" was written by Sonny and Eric Foster White. Its bass line, added by Carol Kaye, made it memorable and enduring. Sonny (1935–98) and Cher (b 1946) had made movies, and worked the night club circuit, building an audience that expanded with the success of the show, the expectant drum roll and masculine announcer's voice building a sense of importance about to happen. Her long black hair, a satiny sheet that neatly fell to her hips and that she would gently pull back from her face with her long painted nails! His moustache! They presented an unusual and strangely compelling duo. Her voice! Deep and loud. Her make-up! Lavish and laid on thick. They looked weird but they looked gorgeous, her tanned lankiness and his energetic compactness. Their clothes were glamorously vivid and interesting and matched each other. Their onstage bantering and bickering made the audience laugh, and made light of irritations that eventually led to their divorce, and the show's demise.

"Teenybopper is our newborn king, uh huh," sings Cher in a line from the song. But the king was really a queen: Cher. She was just out of her teens when she first recorded that line, a young woman navigating patriarchy, attaining her own power despite it and because of it. She's the only artist to have a number one hit single every decade from the 1960s to 2010s, and the oldest female to have one, in 1998 at fifty-two years old, with "Believe."

Cher forthrightly stated in teen magazines that she didn't feel pretty growing up in El Centro, California. Dark-eyed, dark-haired, and olive-skinned, she didn't fit the prevailing standard of beauty: blonde, blue-eyed, pale. The future Oscar winner dropped out of school at sixteen, and sang back-up on the Ronettes's "Be My Baby" (1963) and the Righteous Brothers's "You've Lost That Lovin' Feeling" (1964).

In early clips of Sonny and Cher performing, her clothes provide full body coverage, a contrast to the body-baring clothes she later wore on their hit TV show. Was it because in 1965 Sonny and Cher were kicked out of the lobby of the London Hilton Hotel in England because of the counterculture clothes they were wearing? She's dressed more outrageously ever since.

Joking around in between songs to mostly empty club gigs after the duo lost popularity in the '60s, playfully insulting Sonny, her jokes became the basis for their future and successful comedy show in the '70s. My college chum, Jennie Rosenthal, told me, "I think why Cher was so cool was because … she was very glamorous and very pretty but she also was very self-deprecating." Viewers felt like Cher was one of them—but moreso. "She was over the top but real."

This show would alter the course of Alicia Armendariz's life. The future punk legend known as Alice Bag was a chubby misfit, taunted, who wore white go-go boots as a kid, cherishing her individualism even if it made her lonely and outcast. Born in 1958 at General Hospital in Los Angeles, Alicia was "a daughter of immigrants, from a poor neighborhood, who didn't speak English," she told me. "When I started school, the first message I got was 'You don't belong here.'" Her second-grade teacher renamed her Alice.

Alicia started singing young. "It was the one thing about me that people seemed to like." The first money she ever earned was from singing. Miss Yonkers, her fifth-grade teacher, asked her to sing on an educational bilingual cartoon, and Alicia earned one hundred dollars, more than the monthly rent her parents paid. "Maybe I could be a singer when I grow up," Alicia thought.

Listening to rock music felt like she was finding her way home, she wrote in her 2011 memoir, *Violence Girl: East L.A. Rage to Hollywood Stage, a Chicana Punk Story*, tracing the emergence of her punk rock pedagogy. Alice said her life became stereophonic with artists whose music defied society. "I think punk is bigger than just a musical genre. I think it's really about an attitude and a way of life, and I think the music was … a tool to make the changes that you wanted to see." She told me, "Punk rock is my therapy." Cher didn't sing punk rock, but Cher was different from everyone—from the way she looked to the way she sang. Alicia was drawn to that.

In the summer of 1970, at a march in East L.A. organized by the National Chicano Moratorium Committee to protest the Vietnam War and its drafting of so many Chicano boys and their higher than average mortality rate, Alicia realized she was part of a minority group, felt proud to be part of something powerful, and understood that there were people who wanted to hurt Chicanos (a complex term that felt empowering in the context of organized resistance to exploitation).

But in high school she felt judged by a Chicano activist group she'd wanted to join; her gold platforms, glitter-strewn jeans, and Elton John obsession set her apart. So she switched schools, where she became a cheerleader and performed as Elton Jane in the school talent show, wearing rhinestone glasses, a feather boa, and her highest platform shoes. She wanted to form an all-girl band, like the comic book characters, Josie and the Pussycats.

Alice Bag wearing jeans she customized with Elton John's name. Los Angeles, 1974–5. Photograph courtesy of Alice Bag.

In 1975, when she looked for Elton John and his gold limousine outside the studio where Cher's show planned to have him as a guest, Alicia met Patricia Rainone (who later played in The Gun Club with Blondie's fan club president, singer-guitarist, Jeffrey Lee Pierce; the Sisters of Mercy; and The Damned). The new friends decided to form a band together. They placed ads in *The Recycler*, but mostly guys answered. After drummer Joe Nanini joined the band, and he suggested they wear paper bags onstage, The Bags were born. Alice decorated her bag with cat eyes and lipstick. Her favorite song they did was "Babylonian Gorgon" (1978), written for her by the band's guitarist, Craig Lee. "The lyrics really made me feel seen and the music had lots of space for me to weave in a little more vocal melody than I was typically able to put into our other song," she told me.

Watching and listening to an odd-looking Cher on the musical comedy hour, Alicia Armendariz realized she could live the life she wanted through music. Alice told me that she and her daughter sing Cher songs together today.

♥ ♥ ♥

Jazz experimented with song length and also dissonance, influencing superstar and teen pop idol, David Bowie, motivating the ambitious teen to play saxophone at age thirteen, around 1960. By the end of the decade he'd grown his hair long, picked up a guitar, and written folk tunes. He'd also written 1969's "Space Oddity," a weird and beautiful song that expresses, to me, the feeling of the '60s as it moved into the '70s: sections that sound like different songs play together in one song as the singer launches into space, trying to communicate to planet Earth. The countdown and music sound like taking off, and by the end—a beautiful terrible disconnection.

And I'm floating in a very peculiar way
And the stars look very different today

David sounds like a bed floating in space. The song was released more than once, and a video a few years after the song was written. David, who had studied mime, saw the zeitgeist and flung it back to listeners, upping the ante to stand out. His lightning bolt face from 1973's *Aladdin Sane* album cover is so revered that the image of a red and blue lightning bolt with delicate black lines is its own signifier, reproduced ever since without his face in memes and clothing and advertisements.

Indeed, future Runaways rock star Cherie Currie dressed up as David Bowie when she was fifteen years old, in high school. Her first concert was David's, and she cultivated a look to mimic his. After she was raped, she cut her golden hair. In her memoir, Cherie writes: "Soon my hair will look like David's. I will *be* David Bowie. Beautifully strange. Horribly handsome. I can make myself David Bowie—strong, above the rest, and invincible. And no one will *ever* touch me again." Dressing like David Bowie was a suit of armor for Cherie Currie. She covered her walls with pictures and articles and posters of David. Her twin sister, Marie, colored Cherie's hair with food dye, and drew the *Aladdin Sane* lightning bolt on Cherie's face with fluorescent color make-up pencils.

Another fan who adored David when she was young turned into one of the first Supermodels, Gia Carangi (1960–86), and also one of the first famous women to die from AIDS. When she was a tween she painted her face like David's, too, and the first haircut she ever chose for herself was a copy of David's deep orange spiky-soft locks that he wore on his album cover for 1973's *Pin Ups*. According to Gia's biographer, Stephen Fried, "She and her Aunt Nancy spent an afternoon singing along to Bowie records and perfecting a red lightning bolt from Gia's hairline to her cheek, like the one on the cover of the just-released *Aladdin Sane*." Even Gia's handwriting was affected; she mimicked David's handwriting and word-play from his liner notes for *Pin Ups*. "For Gia, Bowie and adolescence would be interchangeable."

Music writer Gayle Wald told me that "for consumers of teen pop in the 1970s, pop music was a kind of safe place for fantasy, for rehearsing what it might feel like to be in love, or in lust, to work out gender norms and expectations, to find out if you didn't want to conform to those norms and expectations. I think of it as this giant realm of play, which is why it's so powerful." The man who fell to earth and the man who sold the world created an alter ego, too: Ziggy Stardust, a rock star who broke up the band. David, whose half-brother was institutionalized for schizophrenia, would make up characters, then write songs about them and become them onstage. His play with alter egos, dress-up, make-up, high heels, and painted fingernails represents Glam Rock's play with gender roles and sexuality; he had guitar fellatio onstage with guitar player, Mick Ronson. David made it openly cool for boys and girls to switch roles—and share clothes. 1974's "Rebel Rebel" tells us so, and tells us promiscuity could be endearing, too.

> She's not sure if you're a boy or a girl ... Hot tramp, I love you so

The singer's singing style melded the pained countercultural mood with traditional crooning. His absorption of teen pop idoldom can be heard when he dueted with Bing Crosby, wrote a song with riffs similar to a Paul Anka tune that Frank Sinatra sang, and referenced Elvis lyrics in the title of David's 2016 and final studio album, ★. Teen pop stardom is an echoing chamber of mirrors.

David in the 1973 music video for 1971's "Life on Mars?" is sexually objectified the way girls and women are sexually objectified, except he is extraterrestrially empowered. His body fully clothed in a pale blue suit that fits him well, flattering and authoritatively artistic with a shirt and tie of contrasting stripes and a jolt of color, his face in full make-up and in glamorous close-up, orgasmic as he closes his eyes to the guitar playing—a centerfold for outer space. Indeed, the first humans landed on the moon in 1969. David found inspiration all around him, in the art of the universe. Former wife and manager, Angie Bowie, for whom he wrote 1970's "The Prettiest Star," advised him on what to wear in his early days, encouraging his dress-wearing.

The conflicting forces of countercultural equalities and patriarchal domination can be heard in the painful conundrum of the "Wham bam thank you Ma'am" lyric in 1972's "Suffragette City," a line from a jazz song that spells out the patriarchal sexual exploitation of females in a pop song whose title further disses girls and women by attaching the diminishing address of "ette" to a word that represents the serious work of obtaining legal equality. I wonder what David was thinking.

When powerful musicians dressed as women for laughs, such as the Rolling Stones or Led Zeppelin or AC/DC, bands with massive teen fan bases, it reminds me of minstrel shows. A mockery that implies the interest.

A song David co-wrote with former Beatle, John Lennon, 1975's "Fame," sounds like art funk rock with its splatter of sounds, the spaces between the notes a space to dance, and the one-word repetitions spanning four octaves—a teen pop song growing up in the 1970s whose teen idols ponder their fortunes as they write another hit. Star fuckers themselves, groupie aficionados, the rock stars writing about fame, and fame itself, another way to make meaning of life's apparent chaos and mystery.

David, who died from cancer in 2016, made art of his life. He also reinforced the signifiers of teen pop idoldom: crooning in stylish clothes surrounded by girls and women as he represented countercultural ideas via gender, racial, and musical exploration. Gail Ann Dorsey, Black and female, played bass in his band for over fifteen years. He and supermodel Iman from Somalia got married in the early 1990s. Each of his eyes a different color, the star text being that it was from a fistfight over a girl.

♥ ♥ ♥

The Vietnam War ended in 1975, with America bowing out in 1973. Veterans returned to America without much fanfare. It was a war whose tragedies American civilians could actually see because of magazine photos and the news, even if they didn't know anyone in active service. Young people such as myself could see kids my own age—tweens—running naked and crying in the midst of actual war: the destruction, the smoke, and the sorrow. Soldiers in scary uniforms. Napalm exploding and burning flesh. A crying girl running, her arms helpless at her side, naked while everyone else is dressed, and a sobbing boy whose mouth opens in a dark and silent wail, unbearably agonized. The potentially devastating chaos of space, body, and mood was realized in that Pulitzer-Prize-winning photograph by twenty-one-year-old Huynh Cong Ut aka Nick Ut in 1972.

Donny Osmond's "Puppy Love" on the radio in 1972 sounded sweet like flowers and cakes, nothing like that photo that disturbed me so much—until he sang "help me." A cover of a 1959 song written by teen idol, Paul Anka, for teen idol, Annette Funicello, Donny's version sounds like an orchestra of beseeching, with a mature intensity in some of Donny's intonations, like slipping into a verging adulthood. Or awareness: his "help me" sounded scary and real to me.

The Osmond Brothers were a band of very young kids from Utah, Mormons, who began their band in 1960 with Alan (b 1949), Wayne (b 1951), Merrill (b 1953), and Jay (b 1955). Their father, George, loved to sing, and he taught the four brothers how to sing as a barbershop quartet. Donny (b 1957) officially joined the band in 1963, and The Osmond Brothers were hired by Disneyland. They appeared regularly on *The Andy Williams Show* and *The Jerry Lewis Show* during the '60s.

In 1969, Mike Curb of Curb Records encouraged the already popular band to be more like The Jackson 5ive, which they did to great success in 1970 with "One Bad Apple," a song originally written for the Jackson 5ive. By 1970, the band wanted to play rock 'n roll, they'd shortened their name to The Osmonds, and younger sibling Clark (b 1957) had joined the band. I love 1972's "Crazy Horses," a rock song that verges on thrash.

During the '70s, the youngest siblings Marie (b 1959) and Jimmy (b 1963) were added. Older brothers George Virl Osmond, Jr. (b 1945), and Thomas Rulon Osmond (b 1947) were born with hearing challenges and weren't in the band although over the many decades, the two oldest brothers occasionally performed with the band.

The Osmonds had a one-season Saturday morning cartoon bearing their name in 1972. The clothing was hip—vests and bell-sleeved shirts and flared pants. The colors were natural and bright, oranges and greens, and there was merch, too: lunchboxes and dolls, bobbleheads and bubblegum cards. Patches for clothing and accessories. Back then merch seemed like a way to express allegiance. Now it all seems like capitalism to me.

Marie was in charge of Donny's massive fan mail, a huge job as Osmondmania begat Donnymania. The title of 1971's "Go Away Little Girl" alerted little girl listeners that the song was about them. Its cowboy jaunt and Donny's high young voice signal that the song is for kids, or maybe not serious. His voice is lightly echoed and alone among a chorus of female and male voices that sound like adult approval of the rule: no underage sex. But like so many songs sung by '70s teen idols, the song was a cover. Written by the Brill Building songwriters, Gerry Goffin and Carole King, it was first recorded in 1962. The song sounds like a contradiction, a sexy denial that sounds like invitation.

In 1972, Donny appeared in an episode of *Here's Lucy*, a show created by and starring Lucille Ball, a woman who managed to have not just one but three successful incarnations of her 1/2 hour weekly comedy show from 1951 to 1974. In the episode, underage Donny serenades underage Patricia, a character played by Eve Plumb, a Brady Bunch Kid, with a song about not being too young to fall in love, as he falls for the older woman seated beside her. The song he sings, "Too Young," written by Sidney Lippman and Sylvia Dee, was popularized by Nat King Cole in 1951.

Donny's dressed like '70s Elvis, in rhinestone-studded white and a big belt buckle. Mirrored hearts gleamed romantically and playfully on his outfit. Zoey Goto, the author of "Elvis: From Zoot Suits to Jumpsuits," told Megan C. Hills that "Elvis' body-accentuating jumpsuits fell very much within the seductive fashion zeitgeist as men started to occupy the erotic gaze." The '70s mirrored feminism's influence as boys and men became heartthrobs on the covers of magazines and in movies and TV shows geared to females.

From 1976 to 1979, two of the nine Osmond siblings had their own weekly variety show, *Donny & Marie*. Donny and Marie were teens when the show began. The show featured ice skaters and showgirls and guest stars and comedy skits, and showcased Donny and Marie's covers of popular songs and their own originals. The song they sang regularly on the show, "A Little Bit Country, A Little Bit Rock 'n Roll," was written by Marty Cooper and demarcated the duo's difference, a song they sang as a duo, their differences dovetailing. Their lustrous hair, slender bodies, and white-toothed smiles represented an ideal that few, including the siblings themselves, could maintain. Donny, like Sonny in the show he shared with Cher, played the "fall guy," and it was a stigma, said Marie in *Behind the Music*.

Their versions of popular songs sounded smoothed out, each layer like cream, removing all the danger and eros. The pressure of their father's expectations and of being a "one-take Osmond" wore on Donny. His older brothers and younger sister were having hits on the country charts, and his youngest brother was experiencing popularity as a solo artist. But Donny was perceived as uncool. "I was nineteen years old and on the verge of a nervous breakdown," said Donny, a nervous breakdown that found fruition in social anxiety, an anxiety he learned to manage by realizing "I don't have to be perfect anymore," he told *Behind the Music*, and that's how he can do what he loves, which is to perform and play music and sing. "I'm trying to be the person who I really am rather than a concocted image of teen pop idoldom," Donny said.

Marie Osmond was fourteen years old when she had a hit song with 1973's country-tinged "Paper Roses," written by Janice Torre and Fred Spielman. It was her mother, Olive, who suggested she try country music because of the quality of her voice. Marie's voice sounds unwavering and sure, faintly soaring.

Marie wrote a monthly column for *Tiger Beat*. Ann Moses, the editor of the teen magazine from 1966 to 1972, recently posted an article from the *Tiger Beat* archives online. In an article about Marie when she was a tween at eleven years old, Marie details her "Personal ambition: to become a good mother, housekeeper, and wife" and her "Professional ambition: to become a good singer and dancer." This exemplifies the marriage (!) of countercultural values with tradition: a young girl can dream of motherhood *and* a career.

As a young girl, Karen Carpenter (1950–83) dreamed of a career, too. She played the accordion, bass guitar, and flute. She marched in the marching band, beginning with the glockenspiel until she convinced the band director to let her play drums at a time when high school drums lines excluded women. When Karen was nineteen, after a few years playing in jazz trios, she and her brother formed the top-selling musical duo, The Carpenters, a hit-making staple on '70s radio. In many of their songs, Karen of the contralto voice plays drums while she sings. She toured with men and lived on the road, and was a featured interview in teen magazines. She told *Star* magazine,

> People always call me because they think that being a chick drummer, I'm a Woman's Lib fanatic, and *I'm not*! … For myself, when I decided what I wanted to do, I went ahead and did it … I think anybody who has enough self respect and enough brains can do what they want to do … I'm not a successful *girl drummer*, I'm just a drummer that happens to be a *girl*.

♥ ♥ ♥

It's like two turntables. Trying to figure out how to mix songs so they make a whole new song, maybe a better song.

Hip-hop was punk before punk. It was 1973 when an eighteen year old at a block party in the Bronx DJ'd over a spooled beat. DJ Kool Herc was from Jamaica, and legend has it that the party was to raise money for his younger sister's back-to-school clothes—another example of how important fashion is to music. In Manhattan, discotheque DJs worked with two turntables to segue dance tracks so dancers could keep on dancing, and similarly, DJ Herc used two turntables at his recreation room parties.

DJ Herc noticed that dancers at his parties loved the instrumental break when the singer stopped singing. So he extended the break by combining the same break on different turntables: when the instrumental break ended on one record, he began it all over again on the other. This was called a "Merry-Go-Round," or "breakbeat."

DJ Herc lived in Jamaica until he was twelve, when he moved to America, and he knew the DJs in Jamaica toasts (or chants) as the music plays, and DJ Herc toasted dancers, too, some of whom became MCs, or rappers. Dancers were called B-boys or B-girls—"B" for breakdancers. MCs rapped rhymed verses they'd pre-planned or that they freestyled (ad libbed), vocalizing their words in a rhythmic style. DJs were powerful, playing the music for the party, like DJs on radios. MCs were like teen pop idols onstage, often in the middle and up front, commanding attention and moving the party onward with their words.

Bronx DJ, Casanova Fly, was fourteen years old when he attended a DJ Herc rec room party, and heard how loud the music was and observed the sound system and how DJ Herc worked it, and it all made Cassanova Fly want to do what DJ Herc was doing, because "the records that he played would just change the way the party was going," he said in a YouTube clip. DJ Herc didn't get rich from this profound innovation. Powerful radio DJs were white men. Hip-hop made waves without the radio airwaves until (some) radio got fresh; DJs of color commanded their own space outside of radio.

Scratching and breakbeating was original, daring, and musically revolutionary. It takes guts to handle finished products—the stereo, the turntable, the vinyl, the song—and it takes imagination to make something new with it. By the mid-'70s, Grandmaster Flash (b 1958) was spinning two different albums and mixing them. And thirteen-year-old Grand Wizard Theodore originated scratching, or rubbing the vinyl and the needle back and forth together. By the end of the decade, Lady B (b 1962) played hip-hop on a Philadelphia station and became an early hip-hop artist with her 1979 "To the Beat Y'all," and singer Sylvia "Love is Strange" Robbins (1936–2011) organized a rap group, The Sugarhill Gang, for her record label. The Sugarhill Gang became one of the first hip-hop groups to make the radio and the charts with 1979's "Rapper's Delight." The song sampled Chic's 1978 "Good Times," sampling a new way to interpret a song as it's covered.

Creating beats with anything—your mouth, your hand, a table top, two turntables, a microphone; scratching the vinyl by moving the record with your hands for various sounds; mixing the two albums by actually picking up the needle and navigating the vinyl yourself, working with the machine—is a DIY or do-it-yourself tenet. It's hip-hop.

Boom boxes are associated with hip-hop. People made fun of me for carrying around my boom box. I wasn't Black, I wasn't Brown, I was a girl, and also my boom box wasn't big and fancy. But my radio was like air for me, I carried it with me everywhere I went and if I didn't have it I felt bad. I played cassettes, and when the machine ate the tape, I'd carefully pull out the cassette with its long broken strands of tape, then splice the strands together with a bit of clear tape—my own version of resourceful DIY hip-hop punk.

Boom boxes are mobile. I loved that I could go anywhere accompanied by music of my choice. As my editor, Annie

Zaleski, pointed out in her editorial comments as we worked on this book, the mobility of music is striking in an era that meant so much for female freedom. I made my own mixtapes, and listened to those made for me; mixtapes were recordings of various songs from the radio and/or from vinyl records copied together onto one cassette.

The first boom box was born in 1966 (the year I was born!). Like transistor radios (the first one launched in 1954), listeners could carry the music with them. Early radios were heavy, like pieces of furniture, so transistor radios and boom boxes were super cool in their portability. And the music was free, after the initial purchase of the radio. Boys carried boom boxes, but I did, too. In line with the double entendre of teen pop lyrics, I venture forth my own: Music boxes were set free as Second Wave Feminism sought rights and freedoms equal to males.

Second Wave Feminism combined with Sexual Liberation during '70s teen pop can be read in the story of Ann Moses. Born in 1947, Ann grew up in Anaheim, CA. A reporter earning fifteen cents per column inch for the local paper in eighth grade, by senior year she was editor of the school paper, and a member of the Songleading Squad. When she worked for free for *Rhythm 'n' News*, she interviewed music artist James Brown. In her memoir, *Meow! My Groovy Life with Tiger Beat's Teen Idols*, Ann wrote about her work as an editor on the popular magazine, *Tiger Beat*. She began in 1966 with a monthly column, but then she helped decide pin-ups and cover shots, contributed story ideas, and originated new columns. Soon the musicians were contacting her to be featured!

Ann told me that Chuck Laufer got the idea for *Tiger Beat* after a one-off magazine of the Beatles that he'd put out sold out spectacularly, and he wanted to compete with *16* magazine, the popular magazine all about pop stars.

By the time Ann was named editor on her twenty-first birthday, she earned more than her own father, who'd worked at a bank for twenty-five years, and was a vice-president there. She was meeting the teen idols adored by so many, and writing about them and taking photos of them *and* getting that work published. Ann's first lover was Maurice Gibb, a Bee Gee who broke her heart.

In 1972, when Ann found out she was getting paid half what a male counterpart was getting paid at a sister magazine, she quit. *Tiger Beat* offered to double her salary but she and her husband, who'd been earning much less than she and didn't like being referred to as Mr. Ann Moses, believed she was making a stand for feminism by quitting. Years later, Ann found out that her bosses, Chuck Laufer and Ralph Benner, had a nickname for her: Starfucker.

The nickname demonstrates the automatic sexualization of girls and women, and the simultaneous demeaning of them through being sexualized. She rarely slept with any of the musicians! She turned down Roger Daltrey! But even if she had been more sexually active, so what? Ann told me:

> They were very patriarchal. And … the thing that is such a dichotomy is that they very, very soon after I started to work there gave me more and more and more responsibility and every month there would be something else I would take off their plate and I would be responsible for it and handle it all. So they loved the job I was doing. It seemed like it was the times that they would be comfortable making a remark like that and not think anything about it.

The same year she found out about the pay discrepancy, hardcore pornography could be had in movie theaters by women as well as men, and 1972's *Deep Throat*, a movie about a woman with a clitoris in her throat, suggested that oral sex and female orgasms were good even as it seemed insulting to move one female body part to another to guarantee male pleasure and privilege. The film heralded a new outward and public discussion of pornography, creating what was called "porno chic."

When *The Washington Post* journalists Carl Bernstein and Bob Woodward wrote about the Watergate scandal (in which President Nixon was recorded being racist; that he was lying to the American public about breaking into the Democratic National Committee's office where they stole documents and wiretapped; and that he obstructed investigation into the wiretapping) in a series of published articles beginning in 1972, their FBI source was nicknamed Deep Throat. Their research, along with the tape recordings President Nixon had made of his own conversations, led to the president's resignation (the first American president to resign), and to movies about it. One of those movies, a fictional comedy, identified Deep Throat as two teen-aged girls (1999's *Dick*).

Females resonate in the cultural imagination, yet are burdened with sexual responsibility and punished for being sexual while males are not similarly burdened and punished. Why isn't female sexuality ok? And why isn't teen pop taken seriously? Because it's about female desire and romance. The heart shape is a prehistoric symbol of female empowerment and procreation, equivalent to the phallic symbol, according to feminist activist, Gloria Steinem, who says patriarchy trivialized the heart-shaped symbol, a symbol that Donny Osmond wore in shiny abundance on his stage costumes, a symbol the Jackson 5ive wore in their TV show, and a symbol that adorned teen magazines geared to girls.

Gloria wrote that "the heart once symbolized female power. It was a procreative, genital symbol: the female version of the phallic symbol." Fans doodled hearts in their notebooks and lockers, teen magazines and TV shows put heart shapes around the teen pop idol, some girls put a heart atop their i's when they wrote. Teen pop was playful porn for girls and young women, a release, an escape, and a joy. Energy unleashed. Pleasure!

1973–6

"They are having fun," commented my boyfriend as we watched VH1's *Behind the Music* episode about the Bay City Rollers, observing the fans screaming about and running to the band. That was when I realized the basis of fandom: It's fun! It's a community with a shared goal. It's a crush. It's innocent. Or is it? Some musicians are scared of the fans, some do what they can to avoid them. In the VH1 doc, Les and Woody described hiding out in their hotel rooms. The Beatles gave their fans an insulting nickname ("Apple Scruffs"), as has Fleetwood Mac ("punters") and The Who's Pete Townshend ("Track Fans"). Some fans are predatory: a lock of hair, a scrap of clothing. Tears and sweat! So maybe cruel nicknames are a response to that feeling of invasion.

Bell Records executive, Dick Leahy, said when he attended a Bay City Rollers concert to see if he should sign them, he couldn't even hear the music; all he could hear was the "constant screaming" of the fans. He signed the band.

Author and Roller fan Caroline Sullivan remembered trying to meet the band. She told *Behind the Music*: "When I look back on it, the things I remember most are waiting outside hotels with my friends, those Saturday night strategy meetings that we used to have, I mean, the Rollers were … the catalysts, but we, me and my friends, were the real stars."

The band from Scotland who named themselves after an American city was one of the top-selling acts of the '70s. Tartan-clad and bare-chested, the young adult men were faintly adolescent, and looked like cartoon characters, a Saturday morning special in the flesh for budding adolescents. Some of them looked like boys about to be men, and a few of them looked like men, newly formed, which they were. They'd had a weekly TV variety show in England in 1975, named after one of their hit songs on the UK charts, 1974's "Shang-a-Lang." They looked a bit older than American teen heartthrobs, something in the cut of their jawline and the slash of their cheekbones. They got their band name when Alan threw a dart at a map of America and landed on Bay City, Michigan,

Brothers bassist Alan (1948–2018) and drummer Derek Longmuir (b 1951) founded the band with singer Nobby Clark in 1963 when they were tweens and teens. By 1973, guitarists Eric Faulkner (b 1953) and Stuart Wood (b 1957) joined, and Les McKeown (1955–2021) replaced Nobby, and that's the lineup that became famous in the United States. The band's lineup changed again and again as the stress of touring and in-fighting affected individual band members, and by the close of the decade, the band was destined for reunion shows. But at the height of their popularity, which was during '70s teen pop, fans copied their dress by wearing tartan pants and scarves, and songs such as "Saturday Night" (1976), "Money Honey" (1976), and "You Made Me Believe in Magic" (1977) regularly played on the radio. They wore flared highwaters (Roller Strollers!) and multicolored platform shoes and sometimes an open vest over a bare chest. Their hair was flirtily collar-length. Their striped socks and suspenders made them seem playful. "Saturday Night" was so fun! A stutter on the "Saturday" and a chant that sounded like unity! The song was recorded and released in 1973, but it was in 1976, with a new singer, that it became a hit in the United States.

They didn't write many of the songs they recorded, and some have said they couldn't play very well, and it looks like they lip-synced on shows, as many performers did. And perhaps Les lip-synced sometimes to a voice that wasn't his. But the "Titans of Tartan" played well enough to tour and make the charts; they played live on tour and for real on their records, and they looked like boys you might know in high school even though they were excitingly, intriguingly, and romantically from another country. Just listening to "You Made Me Believe in Magic" (1977) feels great, like the person you like just called you on the phone and you talked about nothing but you were really talking about everything. Every sigh a song. Every song a sigh! The happy romance of disco pop with guitar chords, those ascending horns and intimate tones, a ballad to a danceable beat. A song built for fantasy-making, 1977's "The Way I Feel Tonight" sounds like the sex you haven't had yet. A croon something a preteen could rest in, feeling safe but not violated, hopeful and safe in pre-sex splendor.

Listening to them is better than looking at them because to look at them means to understand them in the flesh. Just listening, the grunt and heave of potential abandonment is gone. Innocent, without betrayal or disrespect. And oh! On the TV! Woody gave a wink! Something private for everyone when he winked onstage for the cameras.

But males in bands can be like females—exploited for sexual and financial motives by adults. With '70s teen pop arrives the recognition of the adolescent as powerful and talented but also the sexualization that places their bodies under the control of managers and fans, which makes the performers vulnerable. Band manager Tam Paton told the boys to do illegal stuff such as graffiti for publicity stunts. He lied about a band member's age to make him seem younger. He planted fans and schemes to cause riots at concerts. Tam may have ripped them off, or the accountants he hired did; the Bay City Rollers didn't roll away with much of the money their music, tours, and merch made, despite such a huge success (or a manufactured hype) that it was called Rollermania. Les said Tam gave them drugs to control them, to make them sleep, work, or have sex. In the early 2000s, Ian and Les talked about the sex abuse: Les said Tam drugged and raped him in 1977. Two other band members accused Tam of sexual violence. There are numerous publications, including a book by band biographer Simon Spence that report Tam's abuse of boys in and outside the band.

Tam Paton rifled through Les's hotel rooms, according to Les; Tam took his room key and looked through his personal belongings. Sometimes fans would do that, too. Les and Woody said they hid out in their hotel rooms (which weren't safe from Tam).

When Eric overdosed, Tam called the media *before* calling emergency services.

The child pornography, the car accident that killed someone, the fan who was shot with an airgun on one bandmember's property, the overdose, the police officer who reportedly died soon after a show, the band making scads of money but not receiving much of it, according to several sources including their biography by Simon Spence—all those things wrapped up in the future in the skinny white bodies of boys who looked like the teens they were, on the verge of troubling manhood. The Rollers changed lineups and their name by the late '70s, and various iterations have performed occasionally since then.

Fan clubs hold reunions and karaoke. Seeing and hearing a fan sing along to a Bay City Rollers song at the Rollerfest, on the *Behind the Music* episode about the band, I realized that singing along is a form of community, even if you're alone in your room, and you're not being loud. Or maybe it's communion.

♥ ♥ ♥

Objects have a long history of communion; for example, the Byzantine icons during the Middle Ages which were banned because they were so worshipped. Small paintings on wood panels, the art portrayed saints and holy people. Rubbed smooth by kisses, the depicted icon disappeared. The commandment against idolatry led to their being banned.

From band to brand, the merchandising of pop stars and bands included so many things. So much merch, cultivating fandemonium. Sweatshops and unfair labor practices never occurred to this underage consumer. But still, some kids (such as myself) soon saw the merch (and some of the music) as flimsy and manipulative.

Baseball cards, comic books, magazines, dolls, paperweights, bubblegum, buttons, bobbleheads, blankets, pillows, beach towels, PEZ candy dispensers, lunch bags, and lunchboxes. Posters. Cereal boxes and cereal box records (or flex records, which began in the 1950s). T-shirts, watches, shoes, toys that looked like pets, patches, pin-ups, posters. Pillowcases, which seem especially suggestive: of dreams, of sex.

But I had to have the KISS comic book. My neighbor told me the band's comic book was made from their blood. We both joined the KISS Army. We each got a patch in the mail. He dressed up as drummer Peter and I dressed up as a groupie. My neighbor looked like the kids on the back of 1975's *Alive!* album, two long-haired teens in t-shirts holding up a handmade KISS sign. One teen held up a fist in a rock salute. The band seemed like a present.

The underside of the gift wrapping is the smooth silver and black of the era's cartoon band in platforms, KISS. "You wanted the best, you got the best. The hottest band in the world! KISS!" And with that, the guitar! He's there! Somewhere on the darkened stage! And there! In the light! Rock stars dressed like comic book superheroes, larger than life in their platform boots, dressed to kill in silver and black! The pornography of them, the fantasy of them, the merchandising of them! Scorchmarks on the ceiling that concertgoers could still see a few years later, when they were high school graduates at the graduation ceremony held at the venue KISS played, the Erie County Fieldhouse. My boyfriend—a 60-year-old tattooed Harley biker—tears up when he talks about that concert and describes how he looked up at the scorchmarks at his own graduation.

The fans! Such footage! The rushing! The fire and blood! The explosions and flashing lights! The *band*!

The band formed in 1973's New York City, looking like the down and dirty dreams that fabled city has long represented. Wearing platform boots and Kabuki (Japanese dance-dramas)-style make-up, each member dressed up as an alter ego: singer and rhythm guitarist Paul Stanley (b 1952) as Starchild; singer and bassist Gene Simmons (b 1949) as the Demon; singer and lead guitarist Ace Frehley (b 1951) as the Spaceman; and singer and drummer Peter Criss (b 1945) as the Cat. They were all born in New York, except for Gene, who was born in Israel. They wore all black with silver accents, their faces painted white with black and silver designs. By the early 1980s, Peter and Ace bailed, but during the '70s the original members rocked teen pop as their band admitted the debauchery earlier teen pop idols had denied.

In fact, it was a former teen pop singer, Neil Bogart (1943–82), who signed KISS. He'd changed his last name from Bogatz to Scott to Bogart when he got into the music business, singing songs that made the Billboard Hot 100 such as 1961's teen tragedy tune, "Bobby." Neil earned the name the King of Bubblegum Pop with his promotion of songs such as 1968's "Yummy Yummy Yummy" by Ohio Express when he worked at Buddah Records. KISS was the first band Neil signed to his new label, Casablanca.

KISS embodied an interesting combination of masculine and feminine. Their artistic and sonic expression, similar to their self-presentation, signaled a femininity not usually accepted in boys or men. And they signaled amidst their hard rock songs. My high school friend, Lucie, said: "In the 1970s, the majority of the idols were very feminine. In a way, we're admiring ourselves and what our potential could now be." Gender constructs could bend and meld in this glitter-strewn decade.

In 1975's "C'mon and Love Me," written by Paul, KISS delivers a perfect pop song, and a lot of girlish vulnerability, by referencing magazines and astrology (evident in popular teen mags); the tossings of his long hair in the video clip; and an intonation that sounds vulnerable in its elongation when Paul sings "C'mon."

She's a dancer, a romancer, I'm a Capricorn and she's a Cancer
She saw my picture in a music magazine

Wow! She's got the power of the gaze! And he's self-objectifying—he's in the magazine. But it's the being in the magazine that gives him power, too. Plus, she's got the active verbs in the lyrics!

Paul wears a cape of feathers, long black gloves, bare-chested in silver sprung shoulder straps and form-fitting black, in the music clip that looks like a lip-synced live performance. On the album cover for the song, 1975's *Dressed to Kill*, the band is dressed up in suits—and wearing their make-up and platforms.

Recently I dreamt I dressed up as Paul and it transformed me. I felt powerful and sexually beautiful. No-one could hurt me. I went from being fat and Jewish-looking (in a fatphobic and anti-Semitic culture) to fantastically attractive and strong. I think that's what Paul and Gene did, too.

Paul reasserts his masculinity later in the song: he sings that he's a man, not a baby, and that she looks like a lady. Lady. A word that implies chaste behavior, a required behavior for females in patriarchy, but a word wielded in the song to say a woman can have sex and still be a lady!

Their rock star sparkle appealed to adolescent fantasies; KISS gave me a language for my own fantasies and writing. And Ace! Ace Frehley had silver stars—or something starry—painted over both his eyes, and his black clothes glittered with silver too. His body bowed like a string. He sang on his back, his guitar like a girl on top of him. Paul's lips were pursed in a forever kiss, Peter was mysterious, Gene was monstrous. The band inspired a young generation to rock, inspiring long-lasting adulation. In 2001, after Betty Blowtorch's lead singer and bassist, Bianca, died, she was cremated, and—as per her request—her ashes were put in her beloved KISS lunchbox.

KISS's album covers were often mostly black, or red-striped with Japanese writing, or excitingly all silver. How the band presented themselves made them seem important, and global, their vivaciousness anthemic.

Was KISS bubblegum because they appealed to such young fans with their cartoon personae? Or was it the bubblegum they offered along with their collectible puzzle pieces? The '70s did many cool things, and one of them was to offer a variety of teen pop subgenres. Teen pop, itself a subgenre of popular music, had, during the '70s, its own subgenres, including glam and punk and hip-hop and metal and hard rock. Of the many subgenres that represented teen pop in the '70s, bubblegum is most closely and more immediately associated with teen pop because its teen idols were marketed so clearly as romantic objects for consumers. KISS was hard rock bubblegum pop.

Endorsement of sexual love sounds playful and nonthreatening in another variation of bubblegum pop, Captain & Tennille's 1976 "Muskrat Love," with its title like a kid's cartoon about critters, its cute sound effects, and its musicians dressed up like a movie star and a sailor. The song made grown-up sexual and romantic relationships sound adorable.

Disco, and disco wedded to funk, gave tweens like me more to dream (and write, and think) about. The music gave an auditory glimpse of an adulthood that was glamorous, sparkling, romantic, and celebratory—even in the midst of heartbreak and suffering. Seeing the bands in music clips, and hearing them in movies such as 1976's *Car Wash*, demonstrated what I heard. Chic's 1978 "Le Freak," Parliament's 1978 "Flash Light," and Rose Royce's 1976 "I Wanna Get Next to You" made me—and the entire class of my middle school in Louisville, Kentucky—dance and croon. They are among my all-time favorite songs. Rose Royce's song is so romantic! Chic gave a shout out to swing in their song, and told us to

Find your spot out on the floor

and similarly, "Flashlight" provided a crucial—and countercultural—reminder:

Everybody's got a little light under the sun

Genres such as country gave tweens and teens music, too. Texas-born Tanya Tucker was eight years old when she told her parents she wanted to be a country singer, and at fourteen she had a Top Ten hit with 1972's "Delta Dawn," her low-octave voice convincing for the lyrics about adults. For tweens like me, it was just fun to imitate her warbly voice and pretend we understood the words. Her 1973 hit, "Would You Lay with Me in a Field of Stone?" sounds so serious with its themes of sexual love, responsibility, and doubt, its choruses sounding like adult, angelic, and heavenly endorsement.

♥ ♥ ♥

My college classmate's sister adored teen pop when she was a tween. When she heard about this book, she wanted to talk with me about it. I'd never met her, but our connection was instant. Karen Rolfe and I spontaneously laughed together on the phone when I mentioned that the night before, I'd watched the music clip for The DeFranco Family's 1973 top ten hit "Heartbeat (It's a Lovebeat)." She said, "I don't even know why we're laughing!" "Me neither!" We kept laughing! But then we analyzed it. Karen said, "It's because it's silly." We knew it was silly back then, but it was fun, and we loved it.

"Heartbeat (It's a Lovebeat)," with a thirteen-year-old Tony DeFranco out front as his older siblings sing back up on a stage of brightly colored circles, and dance their practiced and unified moves on it, gives an almost shockingly adult expression. The admiration of youthful bodies becomes idealized and idolized during the 1960s and 1970s, decades that in mood seem to express the emotions of an adolescent, a tween careening into teenhood: clamorous and demanding and pleasure-seeking, some in a conformist rebellion and some in radical individuality, with a sometimes sophistication that confuses adults. The calm that children and kittens have, the casually expressed sensuality of a body in formation that some adults confuse with consent.

The teen magazine *Tiger Beat* featured The DeFranco Family as a way to promote the group's debut record, and the response was so strong that each month the photo of lead singer, tween Tony, got bigger and bigger. In one video clip, the group wears matching patched jeans, and Tony wears a long-sleeved yellow shirt emblazoned with sparkly hearts!

The five brothers and sisters—Benny (b 1953) on guitar, Marisa (b 1954) on keyboards, Nino (b 1955) on guitar, Merlina (b 1957) on drums, and Tony (b 1959) on guitar and maracas—were at first an instrumental quintet playing weddings, banquets, and parades in Welland, Ontario. Their parents, Maria and Antonio, had emigrated from Italy during the 1950s to Port Colborne, Ontario, then to Welland, where they brought up their kids to play instruments in a band together.

Tiger Beat's Chuck Laufer (1923–2011), a publishing magnate, flew them from their small hometown in Canada to Los Angeles to record demos. All except one of the siblings were teens when they scored their hit with 1973's "Heartbeat—It's a Lovebeat," and the oldest, Benny, had just a few months earlier turned twenty. Seasoned studio musicians from The Wrecking Crew played on the cut.

The DeFranco Family featuring Tony DeFranco in the early '70s created music that sounded like the stage sets on which they performed: bright, playful, and organized. They wore matching clothes (that sometimes sparkled!) and danced synchronized moves that were possible to imitate. They performed on several popular TV shows, including *American Bandstand* and the *Sonny & Cher Comedy Hour*. Dancing in front of the TV along with the band as they performed could make a fan feel part of the band. They played their own instruments and sang the songs, too.

Tony told *Your TV History* that the internet got fans in touch with him, and that he heard from women who described that when they were girls, putting his music on the turntable helped them get through terrible childhoods. I can relate! I'm so grateful I had a turntable, and a radio.

Similarly, tweens and teens were also immersed in the teen magazines about teen pop stars. A magazine's influence was important. Covers looked like candy wrappers. Colorful pages acted as promotion for a singer or band, and accompanying text felt serious even when it was fun, superficial, and followed by exclamation points! Any bit of information felt intimate and possibly scandalous! His favorite color was purple! He likes walks on the beach! He loves French Fries! Black and white photos seemed like shared secrets! Questions were enticing. Could you be the girl who understands him? Could you be the girl who rescues him? Would you be the girl to wait for him?

Are you the girl for him?

Teen magazines such as *Tiger Beat* followed a formula: offer a life story in installments, with baby pictures. Sometimes a handwritten note from the star went along with their replies to fan letters in the issue. Usually there was a centerfold. *Tiger Beat* offered promotional gifts after raising the price of the magazine, and ran stories such as "Win a Lock of Donny's Hair!" Was the lock of hair really his? Yes! *Tiger Beat* editor Ann Moses said she tagged along to one of Donny's hair appointments and scooped up some of his shorn locks for the contest.

Many of the magazines were one-offs, or lasted a short time, cashing in on a particular band or musician. Articles with titles from *Fave!* magazine such as "Are You the Girl He's Looking For," "My Special Secret," and "Run away with …" created a titillating intimacy and fantastical potential in its popularly read pages.

Many of the stories were made up, with writers pretending to be the music stars, or pretending to be female. At first, *Tiger Beat* co-founders Ralph Benner or Laudy Powell wrote under the byline of a fictitious sixteen-year-old, Sandi Demming, because Chuck Laufer decided his magazine should include first-person interviews by a teen girl (even if she wasn't real). Musician and SuperGroupie Cherry Vanilla (b 1943) ghostwrote a column as David Bowie for *Mirabelle* magazine from 1973 to 1975 when she worked as his publicist. She told me, "I wrote about all kinds of things, like being on Fire Island, dancing in the waves, Christmas gifts for Angie and Zowie, make-up tips … Anything I was doing/thinking, I made it to be what David was doing/thinking."

"I was David's tongue when it really mattered."

Tiger Beat, founded in 1965, was not the first teen magazine to promote teen pop stars. *16* magazine featured Elvis on its first cover in 1957. Founded by an alleged embezzler, Jacques Chambrun, *16*'s early articles were also written by males posing as females. But then Gloria Stavers (1927–83) became *16* magazine's Editor-in-Chief in 1958, and was so moved by the fan letters from tweens that *16* received that she geared her magazine to them.

Gloria Stavers was influential and derided. Her magazine could make or break a teen pop star or idol, and she wrote many of the features, and took many of the photos. She dated teen pop star Dion (the first fantasy love of SuperGroupie and bestselling author, Pamela Des Barres), and sexualized males in her centerfolds and pin-ups.

In 1971, Chuck Laufer published *Right On!* In 1976, he hired twenty-one-year-old Cynthia Horner as the Editor-in-Chief. Featuring Black artists, the magazine had a deal with The Jackson 5ive to write about them in each issue. Cynthia and Michael Jackson got along, and she and Janet Jackson became friends. Cynthia told *Shondaland*: "Since *Right On!* was an African American publication, we did not get the same type of respect that other publications did. Another challenge, is that when you're really young, people don't want to listen to what you have to say, because they don't think you have the experience to back up what it is you have to say. I was very persistent and determined that my voice was going to be heard." She'd studied journalism in college. They promoted new bands such as New Edition, a teen pop boy band who became popular in the 1980s.

Right On! was similar to other teen mags, such as *Tiger Beat*, with colorful covers like a collage with its cut and paste of headshots and exclamatory words! Something its readers might cut and paste or doodle in their own school lockers, notebooks, or diaries. An assortment of images gave readers lots to ponder.

The Los Angeles-based teen periodical, *Star*, was sometimes referred to as a "groupie magazine" because it featured a few famous groupies. *Star* ran for five issues in 1973; the sixth issue was planned but never published. Until that untimely ending, however, the magazine advocated for female sexual agency and self-empowerment. Articles; contests; groupie comics; "Foxtrology" for astrology; tantalizing rock star centerfolds; interviews with luminaries such as Diana Ross from the Supremes; movie, album, and book reviews; beauty tips; money-making ideas; how-to crafts; and quizzes such as "How Far Out Are You?" harmonized the allure of popular culture with the feeling that one's life can be self-governed, and not only that, exciting and creative.

Star, which sold for fifty cents, was originally geared to girls aged 8–12, spotlighting pop stars David Cassidy and Donny Osmond, before it morphed into what *Star* editorial associate Lori Barth describes as "*Cosmopolitan* for teen-agers."

"The girls went wild," Lori told me, adding, "It was just stuff young girls wanted to read," pointing out that she was a young girl, too. "It was fun to go to work every day … I loved being there." Lori, a songwriter from Sherman Oaks, also managed to perform at venues around LA and eventually earn degrees in history and journalism. "I could work at *Star* magazine in the day, and at night I'd go home and write songs, and record demos," she recalled.

Star's office was located on the famed Sunset Strip in a building with a glass elevator. "I can still picture it," Lori tells me over the phone. "I was there for everything." She was at all the photo shoots, most memorably the one with a naked David Cassidy taking a shower.

When I first spoke with *Star*'s editor, Don Berrigan, he quoted the magazine's tagline: "The girl who reads *Star* is you." Don, who designed the friendly, bold style of the magazine's colorful title and came up with its tagline, told me that he wrote 80 percent of *Star* under various noms de plume—such as Donna Goodbody. He wrote from what he imagined was a girl's point of view. The centerfold of a musician was Don's idea. "Sometimes they'll buy the whole magazine just for the centerfold."

"You gotta go with what's going," Don's mentor, Fred Rice, would say, "so keep your eyes open for what's going, and go with it." For example, *Star*'s logo was a fox, designed and drawn by artist Frank Morton. "'Foxy' was a very important term in those days," Don told me. I told Don that in the "Foxy Lady" forum and letters, it seemed like a feminist revolution was happening, but Don confessed, "I wrote all those letters to provoke the reader." A white man was, perhaps inadvertently and for his own sexual desires, promoting sexual liberation and female empowerment.

Rita Wilson, the actor and powercouple partner of actor, Tom Hanks, modeled for *Star*. She appeared on *The Brady Bunch* in a role where she competed with Marcia for Head Cheerleader ("Greg's Triangle," Season 4, Episode Eleven, December 8, 1972). Roles for girls and women on TV and in real life were traditionally supporting roles: cheerleaders, groupies. But Karen Rolfe pointed out to me that Title IX passed that year, the statute that gave girls room in the sports team not solely outside it.

Rita reportedly quit modeling for *Star* because she thought the magazine was trashy. So that's the crux of countercultural complexity in patriarchy. How can females exist and flourish with the ease that males are allowed? How to be sexual (or not) without feeling or being degraded?

When Don and I concluded our interview, he serenaded me in the manner of early teen pop idols. "Let Me Call You Sweetheart" was written in 1910, with music by Leo Friedman and lyrics by Beth Slater Whitson, but I knew the 1944 version by Bing Crosby. Don's was even better.

♥ ♥ ♥

Alice Cooper made the centerfold in *Star*. Alice, whose shock rock persona created an unusual sex symbol—one made from nightmares—signed to Frank Zappa's record label in 1969. In the March, 1973 *Star* centerfold, he's depicted in a drawing by Petagno with a huge boa constrictor snake, black eye make-up, and a top hat. The eye make-up was influenced by the GTOs, the "groupie group" Frank Zappa produced. Rumor has it that GTO Christine made him cry and that's why he painted his eyes that way.

Alice grew up in Detroit, Michigan, where he was born in 1948. Alice Cooper the band formed in 1964 when Alice was a teen in Arizona, with Michael Bruce (b 1948), Glen Buxton (1947–97), Denis Dunaway (b 1946), and Neil Smith (b 1947). 1971's "I'm Eighteen," written by the band, takes '70s teen pop out of school and romance and into the big world beyond, as far as outer space. Alice—singing in glittery gold pants with a bottle of maybe booze—calls out to his missing mom, does some baby talk, scream-sings his anguish, drops the mic stand, and rubs his Wonder Woman t-shirt-clad belly as he expresses the angst of existence. With gestures from his black-gloved hand to each band member, Alice summons sounds from the instruments they play, a new kind of conductor: make-up smeared and messy and untucked, but just as authoritative.

1972's "School's Out," also written by the band, is an anthem for the ages—all ages, reminding listeners that rebellion is (thankfully) possible at any age. His 1975 solo album, *Welcome to My Nightmare*, offered a model of the sensitive man with his ballad, "Only Women Bleed," a song whose title implies menstruation but whose lyrics offer a possibly sympathetic portrait of women in love with mean men. Women's Liberation in the '70s brought consciousness-raising groups who talked openly about domestic abuse, and in that song a man with a woman's name sings about it.

Alice struggled with alcoholism and drug addiction, and eventually got clean and sober. A friendly golfer by day, by night Alice in concert seemed scary. His theatrical stage shows included monsters, decapitation, and huge bugs; dancers, smoke, and fire fanning the flames of fear. But also relief—it's just a show!

Bands, an expression of abandon, take discipline and practice to express that abandon in a song and on a stage. Humans a vessel of emotions that find reasons for the feelings as it looks around, and find a place to channel it in music—conducting the careen.

A band whose ambition was hidden by the careen of their songs is Sweet. Mike Chapman and Nicky Chinn produced the band, writing their early bubblegum pop songs, such as 1972's "Little Willy," which sounds like a schoolyard chant with dirty lyrics. "We want the Sweet" chants the audience on 1973's "Teenage Rampage," in contrast to the band-hating audience who caused a riot at a 1973 concert at Grand Hall Palace Theater in Kilmarnock, Scotland, an audience that may have inspired Sweet's 1973 "Ballroom Blitz," a song that became a hit in the United States in 1975, a song that sounds like an explosion. Punk! Glam! Rock! Bubblegum Pop! Grown men—obviously grown men with their fleshy thighs and facial hair, they were all nearing 30 by the mid-'70s—acting like kids and looking like women with the furious ambition of the dedicated musician! Sweet gave it all to us.

At first, studio musicians played for them, but then they played for us. During the '70s, the band lineup included men from Scotland, England, and Wales: singer Brian Connelly (1945–97); bassist Steve Priest (1948–2020); guitarist Andy

Scott (b 1949); and drummer and vocalist Mick Tucker (1947–2002), all of whom co-wrote and actually played on 1974's "Fox on the Run"—a song about a groupie, and one of my all-time favorite songs, and one I've wedded to my vegan ecofeminism. The song was a US hit in 1975.

Sweet's teen pop had an adult edge; the lead singer sounded mature. One of their concerts reportedly had a huge prop penis ejaculate confetti during the show. But their songs sounded excitingly outside age, and let listeners in on the action; singer Brian called out to the bandmates by name. Sometimes, the singing sounded like a caricature. A lot of the singing had echoes, and sound effects, distant or close up, way high or down low, smooth or warbly. Each layer and passage was like a new character in a movie, or a new way to express a thought or feeling. 1978's "Love Is Like Oxygen," the first vinyl album that I bought with my own money, sounded weird and cool. The singer sounded ageless and genderless in the song, and eerily meaningful. It sounded like life lessons, the title itself a lesson. Love is like oxygen.

Simple, laughable. But how true the words. And it was how the music sounded, how the singing sounded—energetic, velvety soft or slurry or like pulled strings, voices and beats in the song sounding almost out of control. There was a lot of variety in a Sweet song—different timbre voices, different rhythms of lines, slow and fast passages. I listened to it often and it felt like something beloved, it felt like cinema.

> I walk the streets at night
> To be hidden by the city lights, city lights

I'm not sure I understood a lot of the lyrics in the songs that appealed to me in the '70s, but I wonder if it matters. The song made meaning for me with its sounds, and the occasional line

I did comprehend. Anyway, the song was jaunty yet cool, not juvenile, which is how some teen pop sounded! It's what kids (everyone?) are reaching for—what's beyond this life in my room, at home, at school, my street? Where is this sound on the radio, my turntable, actually coming from? A distant planet, a lonely star—something tweens and teens could hitch their stickered wagon to.

Lavender satin! Shiny silver! Glamorous gold! Evening black! The band members like sophisticated candy bars in fluorescent colors. The men in the band looked theatrical like women and looked playful like kids with their long hair and eye-shadow, their platform shoes and face stickers and body glitter.

Sweet's Glam look was taken even further by the piano prodigy who became a knighted superstar, Elton John, who'd astonished his family when he played music by ear on the piano at the age of three, and in the '70s astonished audiences with his glitter-scattered, feather-filled, opulently colorful stage personality. He began his long-time songwriting collaboration when he was twenty, in 1967, with a seventeen-year-old songwriting partner, Bernie Taupin, a partnership that would make the duo millions and a legacy for the musical hereafter.

Elton John's music and outlandish appearances—songs he wrote and played, sparkling clothes with a sense of humor, his signature and often over-sized tinted sunglasses, and the stage performances he envisioned—appealed to tweens, teens, and adults; his songs of sensitive drama or fun narratives made listeners want to listen, dance, and sing along. His stage-show's unique theatrics (Elvis impersonators; an introduction by *Deep Throat*'s porn star, Linda Lovelace; a Beatle onstage; faux gem-encrusted outfits; platform shoes) along with his sophisticated yet accessible songs propelled Elton to superstardom. His music sounded like an amazing soundtrack to the amazement of living.

Sexuality in the '70s was experimental and sparkling, but the gender binary and heteronormative pressure kept many in the closet, and many adamantly performative of a masculinity identified with heterosexual activity, for example, hetero marriage. Linda Hannon née Woodrow told "Good Morning Britain" that while she and Elton planned to marry, she supported Elton and Bernie, and bought the engagement ring. Then one night Elton came home at 4 am and said the wedding was off, just like in his 1975 song, "Someone Saved My Life Tonight." Elton was saved by not getting married. Hopefully Linda was, too.

1976–9

Elton John's lyrics expressed adult concerns in music tweens and teens loved. Heart also made music for adults that a youth market adored.

A hard rock band who formed in 1973, sisters Ann and Nancy Wilson were the heart of it. Born in 1950 and 1954, respectively, Ann Wilson's soprano-range voice and Nancy Wilson's guitar-playing got listeners used to hearing women rock out on the radio, on TV in music videos, and onstage during the '70s. Their 1977 song, "Barracuda," defiantly responded to patriarchy's insistence on sexually objectifying them. The album cover for their 1977 album, *Little Queen*, showed them tough and on tour, the center of the frame, the men mere backdrops. Heart intrigued me so! They opened up hard rock and the road beyond groupies and male musicians. In their memoir, they said they didn't want to marry the Beatles, they wanted to *be* the Beatles.

1975's "Dreamboat Annie" is a delicate road song, relentless and soothing as the sisters set forth in the diamond winds with their band.

> Heading out this morning
> Into the sun

Heart sisters set their course. Every time I hear and see the 1978 concert footage of Heart performing their 1975 single, "Crazy on You," I know I'm watching feminism in musical action. Ann wields her voice and Nancy her guitar as powerfully, and as powerfully sexy, as any man, the entirety of their bodies unfettered by self-conscious constraints.

Similarly, Fleetwood Mac appealed to the youth market, especially lead singer Stevie Nicks, with her voice that sometimes goes beyond gender and her songs that sometimes go beyond genre and her style that created an iconic look. Stevie is the mentor, the aunt, your older sister's friend whom you are so fucking happy is nice to you, her words like gold, the alchemical witch. Her witchy layers, glittering and gossamer, her awkward ballet moves endearing, a style fans emulated. She's reaching for the stars just like you, you teen tween ageless soul, and she turned herself into a star, too. Sure, another thin white girl with a small nose and a pretty smile and flying blonde hair, but … something to find in her that's resonant.

Fleetwood Mac originally formed in London, 1967, but during the '70s their blues rock turned more melodic, and its mysterious harmonies became associated with California cool, the '70s, and Stevie. She was born in Arizona in 1948, joined a folk band in high school, and after she met guitarist, Lindsey Buckingham (b 1949), by harmonizing with him at a party, he asked her to join his band, and later they worked as a duo.

Buckingham Nicks joined the respected band Fleetwood Mac in 1975, with Stevie laying down her music and words onto a cassette that she gave to Lindsey to produce. With 1975's "Rhiannon," a song about a legend became a legend with its otherworldly and knowledgeable intonation; it sounded as though Stevie was sharing powerfully mystical knowledge with you, the band sounding like forces of nature she summoned. Stevie takes power via her narrative omniscience. Fans dressed the way Stevie dressed, and Rhiannon became a popular name for girls. Stevie turned the once-insulting (and sometimes fatal) female-identified label of "witch" into a long-living compliment.

Nevermind the boring concert clips; the band looked cool on their album covers, and on the cover of *Rolling Stone*, in bed and in a band together. The cover of the band in bed was shot by Annie Leibovitz for a 1977 issue, and it made clear the band made music together on every level. Stevie—and pianist, singer, songwriter, Christine McVie (1943–2022), notably with 1977's beautiful *Songbird*—made it clear that what was ahead for us girl tweens and teens was not just a man. There was the real and metaphorical wedding—both were involved with men in the band, and Christine was married to bassist John, and *Songbird*'s lyrics are biblical in their loving generosity to a mate—but the bridal gown was not the end of the fashion show. Their music, music they made with men, showed women could live and create and partner with musicians, as equals—or as much equals as can be in a violent patriarchy. Were the rumors that Lindsey hit Stevie true? In 1981, Stevie created a successful solo career.

Their songs, like ABBA's, sounded like they were preparing the tweens and teens who listened to them for the adulthood the band sang about, that pain and suffering could be endured and maybe transformed.

ABBA's song about a seventeen year old, 1976's "Dancing Queen," described something a tween could live for. The adult singers of the songs appealed to a tween and teen market as well as to adults. The music sounded like silver velvet and the sheen of musical instruments and lovely voices amidst layers of deep orange satin. In "Dancing Queen," ABBA sang about youth, and how young love and joy, desire and dancing can make us feel. Excitingly and powerfully, in a gesture that discards the emotional (and monogamous) baggage put upon girls and women in so many songs, the dancing queen gets to dance with as many partners as she likes:

> Looking out for another, anyone will do
> You are the dancing queen

Looking more adult than teen pop stars because they were adults, ABBA's members were all born between 1945 and 1950, making the youngest member 24–5 and the oldest 29–30 when they first climbed the US charts. Benny Andersson, Agnetha Fältskog, Frida Lyngstad, and Björn Ulvaeus were from Australia, and won the esteemed Eurovision Song Contest in 1974 with "Waterloo" soon after winning America's dancing heart. As Elisabeth Vincentelli said, ABBA was a "worldwide superstar band."

Dressed in blue satin jumpsuits and gold boots and animal-print edged robes and silver dresses and tinfoil, costumes by Owe Sandström made the band look like kids playing dress-up, which appealed to kids like me, who liked to play dress up. I liked their satins and pornographic make-up—tweezed eyebrows and blue eyeshadow. Dancing as a substitute for sex meant tweens and teens were allowed.

Youth cool brought a teen-aged Joan Jett to Rodney's English Disco in the '70s, a popular teen hangout on Sunset

Boulevard in Hollywood, California. She wore a look inspired by singer and bassist Suzi Quatro, copying her choppy hair and glam-rock clothes. Joan befriended the club's owner, DJ Rodney Bingenheimer (b 1947), who promoted female musicians even as he reportedly requested sexual favors in exchange. Joan hung out at clubs, including his, looking for girls around her age to join the band she wanted to start. Joan's teen dream came true when she co-founded The Runaways. The band signed with a major label, released four albums, and toured the world. Cherie Currie, who auditioned for the band with a rendition of the jazz/r & b song, "Fever," created an iconic look with her bleached blonde short feathered hair, and her corset with garters and bikini underwear, when she sang onstage in a stance like a Sheela na gig, legs bent and spread like an unashamed rock star. Sheela na gigs were architectural renditions of female forms with open vulvas, often built over doorways and windows of churches or castles as protection.

The Runaways, an all-American teen band (with a lead guitarist from England), debuted at an influential club in West Hollywood, the Starwood, in 1975. Each band member based their manner on a rock star, according to Jackie Fox in the 2004 documentary, *Edgeplay*: Singer Cherie Currie (b 1959) emulated David Bowie; lead guitarist Lita Ford (b 1958), Ritchie Blackmore and Jimi Hendrix; singer/guitarist and bassist Jackie Fox (b 1959), Gene Simmons; Joan Jett (b 1958), Suzi Quatro; and drummer Sandy West (1959–2006), probably Roger Taylor. The original bassist was Micki Steele (b 1955), but she soon left the band and eventually joined the popular 1980s band, The Bangles. Bass players were, in order of replacement, Peggy Foster, Jackie Fox, Vicki Blue, and Laurie McAllister. Kari Krome, the band's co-founder and songwriter, signed on when she was a teen but soon quit the band because band manager Kim Fowley (1939–2015) was so creepy and abusive.

Jackie Fox stated that the reason she ultimately quit the band, too, was because Kim Fowley raped her. Jackie alleged that Joan and Cherie were in the room that New Year's Eve night in 1975 and did nothing to stop the rape. The Runaways officially broke up because of musical disagreements in 1979.

Their debut single, 1976's "Cherry Bomb," is a teen-age anthem obliterating the teenage blues it sings about—a coming out to parents, and to the world. It announces a realization that the individual can have a life beyond the control of family and school. Sandy's drum rolls it out at the exciting start of the song, and Cherie proclaims:

> Can't stay at home, can't stay at school
> Old folks say, "You poor little fool"

Then she says she's the girl next door, a fox to wait for. A self-assertion that is as much defiant as it is sexual, it sounds aggressive. The band looked like the cool girls I really wished I could be. They looked like a gang. Youth gone wild.

There's a lot to analyze in the song: moaning sounds sexual; there is the stuttering on the word, "cherry," which is slang for hymen (the sometimes present tissue of skin at the vaginal opening, culturally symbolizing though not actually always indicating virginity); plus cherry bombs are explosive devices or fireworks in the red round shape of the cherry fruit, and their original powder composite was banned in 1966, with the cherry bomb law passing in 1977; and the lyric about having and grabbing and making someone sore. Just what is going on in the song? Teen sexual desire during Second Wave Feminism. And, some of the band members liked girls and women sexually and romantically. But also, the band was managed by an alleged rapist man.

Female sexual aggressiveness in "Cherry Bomb" allowed girls and women a freedom and fun not previously allowed (or admitted) in earlier generations. Fishnetted and high-heeled, corsetted in white satin with black stitching and bleached in blonde, daringly sexual in a patriarchy whose legislation tries to control reproduction and pays women less for equal work, and sex work is the only work where girls and women earn more than boys and men, a culture in which girls are trained to never say "no" or "I" and boys are trained to ignore "no" and be the primary "I," The Runaways exploded ideas about masculine and feminine because they were both. It's a reckoning the band lived.

1977's "Waitin' for the Night," which features Joan singing lead after Cherie's departure from the band, sounds like a power ballad, those songs usually sung by men. It's especially poignant for me because it's girls singing. Teen girls. Teen girls who didn't look like prom queens, cheerleaders, or supermodels. They looked like the girls in my junior high school—sure, the girls who didn't include me in their gang because I was too fat and too goody goody and plus I rarely showed up at school anyway, but girls who, with their wild hair, slutty eyeliner, and leather jackets, gave me an alternative to preps, cheerleaders, and normies. How I love the way they stood. Tough and sexy. Cocky. Cocksure. *Cunty. Cuntsure.*

Listening to the all-girl band is like hearing a conversation you want to join instead of just overhearing it.

In footage of 1978's song "Saturday Night Special," The Runaways look so … I need a new word to replace "masculine," one that integrates the gender constructs of masculine and feminine. It's that every band member has a musical part and they play it with strength. I'd like to sing back-up like lead guitarist Lita, her voice flowing like her long hair.

> You do what you want to, let's see what you've got
> And if I don't like it, I can tell you to stop

♥ ♥ ♥

An album cover that emphasized the power of the female gaze and that was also layered with social signifiers of sexual orientation is 1979's *Room Service*. Teen pop idol Shaun Cassidy, wearing a ribbed tank top and jeans as he stands, turned away from the mirror and a TV on a dressing table in what looks like an anonymous hotel room, smiles so openly as a voyeur peeps in at him that certainly no harm can be done! Is the voyeur male or female? S/he is in shadow. The album title's play on words confounds any sense of potential violation, complicating invitation and violation. It's an album cover that addresses the gender play of the '70s—and the age-old issue of consent.

And power play. Feminized teen pop stars meant female fans could identify as well as objectify. '70s teen pop devotee, Karen Rolfe, told me:

> I remember in those magazines … you could win a contest and meet Shaun Cassidy. So in my mind I win the contest. I go to the concert, and after the concert, they set us up to go to a cabin, and it's snowing … Secretly, I have a terrible voice, but I always wanted to sing, and we're singing to each other, and I'm sure we made out. I don't know if it went further than that but I won the contest … and I suddenly have a good voice.

Photographs of their teen pop doodles courtesy of twin sisters, Cindy and Allison Wolfe, Mt. Vernon, Washington 1976.

Television appearances promoted his teen idoldom, such as Shaun's long-running presence on the TV series, *The Hardy Boys*, in which he co-starred with Parker Stevenson from 1977–9. Shaun and Parker were featured on the covers and in the pages of many teen magazines, bringing the casually appealing young men with floppy hair into the hands and homes of viewers, some of whom were already crushing on the stars. For viewers with TVs in their bedrooms, watching the show felt more intimate and private. Reading a magazine in bed felt cozy. With his feathered yellow-blonde hair and friendly smile, Shaun looked like the younger brother he was in real life and on the series—more innocent, less complex, vaguely athletic. He sang on the show, as he and his TV brother Parker solved mysteries.

Born in 1958 to Shirley Jones and Jack Cassidy, which made him David Cassidy's younger half-brother, Shaun played in a band as a tween. The Hollywood, CA-born Shaun released his first album when he was nineteen. His first US hit was 1977's "Da Doo Ron Ron," an earlier hit for a girl group, The Crystals and their fifteen-year old lead singer, La La Brooks, in 1963. Shaun named his second album *Born Late* (1977), a title that could appeal to tweens and teens in its grasp of mental sophistication before bodily maturity, a youthful confidence that believes itself more mature than its years lived. His satin baseball jackets! His skin-tight stage clothes of shining black! His innocent strength. That reassuring smile that could advertise anything wonderful at all! The popular jock who might actually like you.

Sports-playing was implied in the clothing of teen pop stars in the late '70s. Andy Gibb also wore satiny baseball jackets (sometimes with nothing underneath!) when he wasn't wearing soft-flowing shirts in smooth and soft materials. The popular fashion suggested the physicality and sensations possible, and gave non-jocks like myself an excuse to wear the comfortably casual jackets, too. Mine was gold-glittered.

Andy was born in England in 1958 to musical parents—his mom had sung in a big band, his father, a bandleader and drummer. Raised in Australia, Andy admired his three older brothers, Barry and twins Maurice and Robin, who were the popular musicians, the Bee Gees. Andy made his musical debut at age thirteen and dropped out of school at fifteen to be a musician. When he was eighteen, he released *Flowing Rivers* (1977), an album of country-tinged pop and balladry that yielded smash hit singles, and followed that up with the dance-friendly love songs of the chart-topping success, *Shadow Dancing* (1978).

1977's "I Just Want to Be Your Everything," written by Andy and Barry Gibb, might deliver co-dependent lyrics but its lively beauty feels so happy, a song whose rhythm for fast dancing works just as well slow. His voice sounded fun. It was on the radio almost every time I turned it on as Andy became a superstar teen idol. When Andy made the charts, and was the first solo artist to attain three consecutive number one singles, the Bee Gees were achieving more fame and acclaim than they had when he was a kid—in fact, oldest brother, Barry, wrote four songs that were consecutive number one hits (a song for Andy, a song for Yvonne Elliman, and two for the Bee Gees). The Gibb brothers created pop song perfection, a dance song confection. Merch included jigsaw puzzles, a plastic guitar, and a heart-shaped paperweight (which I still have).

Written by Barry Gibb and Blue Weaver, Andy's 1979 "(Our Love) Don't Throw It All Away" is heartbreaking. It's a tween teen dream come true, too. Its romance feels youthful and yet sophisticated. There's an innocence to the desire in a voice and melody that sound sweet yet mature.

1978's "Waiting for You," written by Andy, was my favorite song. It sounded like a secret I didn't want anyone to hear, and made me blush to hear it. Andy's voice and words are so heartfelt. It's like he's made of clouds and gold and gallantry.

♥ ♥ ♥

Another sound that was sweetly sophisticated then is 1978's "Heart of Glass," written by Debbie Harry and Chris Stein, which told listeners something new to me when I was twelve: that females could get bored with boys. And cuss in a song!

> Once I had a love and it was a gas
> Soon turned out to be a pain in the ass

Debbie's cool voice, cool tone, and cool clothes made it seem like girls could be as cool as boys—and not victims. In the video, her gossamer gown and creamy white eyelids and mirrored ball and disco lights flashing create a shimmering strength in heartbreak. What a star!

The cover of 1978's *Parallel Lines* intrigued tweens like me. I ate every song like glass candy—it crunched but went down smooth, like power pop. The cover was clever: an unsmiling woman in a white dress stands in high-heeled peep-toe mules in front of a band of suited men in black ties, and the background is black and white. She looked tough and sexy and stylish, with black and white hair. She reminded me of my Tiffany doll, whose hair could be blonde or brunette but was usually both. The band didn't like the bubblegum pop style of the cover, but this tween sure did. A punk band with three disco hits by the end of the decade, Debbie's punk élan and her own band was glamorous feminism.

A besotted fan ran the band's fan club and formed his own band, too, demonstrating that gendering fandom as female is inaccurate, and that the '70s challenged limiting gender constructs.

Debbie (b 1945) was about thirty when she formed Blondie in New York with her boyfriend, guitarist Chris (b 1950), in 1974. By the end of the decade the lineup had included Clem Burke (b 1955) on drums, Jimmy Destri (b 1954) on keyboards, Frank Infante (b 1951) on bass and guitar, Nigel Harrison (b 1951) on bass, and Gary Valentine (b 1955) on bass. The name of the band came from catcalls the singer received, and as with her cheesecake photos and song lyrics, Debbie subverts the sexism with her tough girl eating candy vibe.

Not teen-agers anymore but with an ear to the radio as much as any music-enamored teen, Blondie made songs that combined various genres: punk, pop, disco, rap. Born in Miami and raised in New Jersey to adoptive parents, Debbie dreamed of being Marilyn Monroe's daughter, wanted to wear black turtlenecks at the age of eight or nine, was voted Best Looking in high school, then waited tables in NYC at Max's Kansas City after taking college classes. Her sense of humor, streetwise sexiness, and to-the-point phrasings have saved her—and everyone who listens. She says the only thing she regrets is that she can't wear high heels anymore.

One night in the early '70s, a man followed Debbie and Chris, forced them at knifepoint into their apartment, tied them up, and stole their gear. The man raped Debbie. She told *NME*:

> Well I think it *did* affect me. I think I have a bit of a stubborn will to survive—for good or for bad. I mean, it could have turned out badly but it didn't so I think one has to have a sense of relativity. I think you can really hurt yourself by carrying around a lot of fear and I realised early on that fear is destructive.

I loved Blondie. I learned all the lyrics to their songs. The singer was impossibly beautiful, but because she seemed older, not a teen, her beauty was more like a distant promise rather than a nearby indictment. Around that time I wore a red wraparound skirt as a dress along with black striped stockings and walked up and down a popular road in my small town. I thought I was being creative and bold, like Debbie Harry or Cher, different from the standard, and proving my escape from a painful childhood. But my cousin told me years and years later that she saw me out walking that day in the late '70s, and that she'd thought, "There's something wrong with that girl." I felt so shamed. Recently watching Debbie Harry wearing an unusual outfit in the music clip for "Dreaming" makes me feel less bad about my tweenage daring-do. Her sneer of a smile! Sure, Debbie had great beauty and a band and a stage and NYC. But I'm understanding more than ever how daring difference is crucial for creativity—and democracy—in daily life.

"Dreaming," written by Debbie and Chris, climbed the charts in 1979, a teen pop song for adults, too. Debbie Harry at the end of the decade, like Alice Bag in the middle and Cher at the start, gave us all something that society struggles to allow: uniquely individual creative expression.

Debbie told *Behind the Music*: "What we were doing was a political statement and I felt that the idea of being in a rock band was part of being somewhat revolutionary, and doing something that was a countercultural kind of thing, but also a progressive thing." Blondie took counterculture further by combining punk, hip-hop, and disco. "We were all pretty much self-taught, and we learned from experience and from listening to records." Debbie and her band forged an alliance between punk's and hip-hop's DIY ethos and disco's sheen. Disco at heart might be bubblegum pop with a funkier groove and a social message—dancing on the dance floor a lot like how a body moves through society.

The day *Roe* v. *Wade* was overturned, I e-mailed teen pop star and working musician Suzi Quatro. The bassist, singer, and songwriter represents the evolution of feminism and gender roles in a '70s culture reckoning with liberation, equality, and freedom. In 1973, Suzi appeared as a *Penthouse* centerfold—fully clothed. By the end of the decade, she guest-starred in the hit TV series *Happy Days*, a popular show set in the 1950s, playing a rock 'n roller—placing herself firmly in the story of rock and how it's perceived.

Suzi played the part of Leather Tuscadero on the TV series. Leather was unlike most females on TV, being a musician, and her older sister on the show, Pinky, also challenged gender conventions by being a mechanic. Pinky dated motorcycle-riding Fonzie, who rented a room at the Cunninghams, a family whose teen daughter, Joanie, joined Leather's band. The Fonz managed the band. They sang one of Suzi's songs on the show, 1974's "Devil Gate Drive," singing about teens, queens, and jukebox scenes.

Suzi looked like a badass bolt of satin when she stood on stage with her bass and blunt haircut, shaking her hips and singing into the mic. She represented a female musician equivalent to male musicians with her instrument in her hands and her leather-clad body in promo photos of her in a one-piece body suit, with a zipper that went from her chest all the way down. Her mentor, Mickie Most, came up with the idea of a jumpsuit. Suzi suggested leather.

With feather-flipped hair, ropes of necklaces, and big rings on her fingers, she looked like the cute bad boy smoking Marlboros out back of the school, a thrill of danger just in the way he stood. But the cute bad boy was a girl.

Suzi picked up the bass when she was fourteen and joined her sisters' garage rock band, the Pleasure Seekers, an all-female band. She dropped out of school to play. She'd loved music even before that; when Suzi was around six to eight years old, she played bongos for her father's jazz band. Born in 1950 Detroit, Michigan, the fourth of five children, and raised in a local suburb, Suzi told me that she "worked at my craft from age 14, doing a tremendous amount of live work, five sets a night in clubs," and that it was very hard. But "it was worth it," every sacrifice she made was worth it. In 1971, music producer Mickie Most approached Suzi to go to England and go solo, which she did. Her first international solo hit was in 1973 with "Can the Can," followed by several hit songs in the UK. In 1978 she attained international acclaim again with the radio-friendly hit song, "Stumblin' In."

I asked her how she's survived. She's worked as a musician for fifty-eight years! She said that she processes pain by feeling it, then writes "either a song or poem about it." Suzi said she was all about the music. "I don't need to get high to do what I do," she wrote. "I have always insisted on being me … whatever that may be, and what I was was not normal, and had not been done … I refused to be somebody else's version of me. My stance is natural, my look is natural." She said she was a tomboy, and had a nonthreatening sexuality, innocent in that leather jumpsuit that is her signature.

I asked her, "What is a groupie?" Suzi said, "Somebody who would lay down their life and body for you!!!" I asked her if she had groupies. "Sure, if you don't you're not famous! I have groupies of both sexes."

♥ ♥ ♥

Some teen pop idols found musical work on another kind of stage—Broadway. Rex Smith debuted on stage in the 1978 production of *Grease*. In 1979, his hit single "You Take My Breath Away" put him in the heart-shaped lockets of tweens and teens. Indeed, on the album's back cover, a young girl wears a necklace with a heart-shaped locket, and it's open to reveal the face of Rex. The album included the soundtrack for the made-for-TV movie, 1979's *Sooner or Later*.

Young boys who had long hair were allowed to dance because they looked like girls and they were musicians on a stage—a spectacle. Rex's body was more grown-up—he was playing a seventeen year old in the movie when he was twenty-four. Denise Miller was sixteen when she co-starred in it, playing a thirteen year old.

Teen Beat, which began in 1967, splashed dramatically enticing titles about Rex on its covers, such as "Rex Reveals: 'My Love is the Only Thing I Have to Give,'" along with a contest that promised readers "could win the shirt off Rex's back." The teen idol magazines offered games, astrology, make-up tips, crafts, contests, articles, and fiction along with a nifty subversion of *Playboy*'s tagline, "Entertainment for men."

Playboy, a magazine that began in 1953, featured naked women alongside ads and articles, and a centerfold of a naked woman accompanied by a questionnaire (answered in her own handwriting) that read like a product manual. But entertainment for men turned into entertainment for girls when teen magazines featured their own suggestive covers and centerfolds. Teen magazines put boys and men in the middle of magazines, and girls and women in the middle of the story.

"And all of a sudden, it's a song! A song they've built around me and my four chords—the four chords Michael taught me. Me and my four chords are the star of this song." So writes the adolescent narrator of the 1978 novel, *Sooner or Later*, which begat the film of the same name, in which thirteen-year-old

Jessie meets seventeen-year-old Michael at the local mall, where he and his band are performing. She puts on make-up and takes guitar lessons from him. They fall in love, and he is her first sexual experience.

They're sitting on his car at a party where all his older, more experienced friends are watching when he invites her to share the stage with him. She nervously joins him. "I reach out and grab my guitar case, at the last minute," and then she plays guitar. As she plays onstage with his band, the Skye band, Michael sings the lyrics he wrote for her. Tweens like me were reading about an older boy musician sharing his musical knowledge, his body, and the stage with a younger girl fan who wanted to be more than underage.

An underage person is not yet considered an adult by law, and adults by law are not allowed to have sex with underage people. The legal age of consent varies from state to state, and has changed over the years. Age differences between the people having sex, the gender, the type of sex, and whether or not one person is an authority or trusted figure also affect the determination of consensual and legal sex. The laws also vary per state. Legal competency to consent is the foundation of the laws regarding consensual sex. By 1900 and through today, the legal age of consent is 16–18 in most states. "Underage" refers to people under the legal age of consent. The word itself can be imbued with a musical resonance of sexual danger that's appealing in its first-time excitement. It's the true consent that matters, though.

Menudo were a band of underage boys. In the '70s, Menudo Fever was the high-energy money-making popularity of a boy band from Puerto Rico who reached international fame when, in 1985, they made the US Billboard charts with "Hold Me." Menudo owned their own private jet, their name emblazoned on each side. Menudo Fever reestablished the boy band mania that began with the Beatles in the 1960s, and that would help codify teen pop.

Organized by Edgardo Diaz in 1977 when he was thirty years old, Menudo were originally two brothers: Fernando and Nefty Sallaberry, and Edgardo's cousins, Carlos, Oscar, and Ricky Meléndez. Menudo covered popular songs of artists in Spain, bringing the songs to Puerto Rico; performed in talent shows; recorded TV jingles; and played local festivals. They wore the international symbol of teen cool: blue jeans. And also the uncool: neon formfitting wear. They were photographed at pools and in their swim trunks.

According to the mini-series documentary, *Menudo: Forever Young* (2022), each band member was replaced when they were too old for Edgardo, for a total of almost forty band members during twenty years. They were all under sixteen, and as young as nine. Parents had to sign a contract that relinquished custody of their sons over to Edgardo. The boys were replaced by younger members when their voices deepened. Some have said they were talked to by management in sexualized ways, exposed to drugs and alcohol, and raped.

They weren't so nice to each other, either, acting out like cruel fraternity brothers with hazing and dangerous bullying.

So what happens when boys are treated like girls— as sex or romance objects? The same thing, it turns out: giddy explorations and musical expression and fun and sometimes a lot of money made. But also: exploitation, sexual harassment, rape. Being ripped off and unprotected. Punished for serving, in any language. When boys are objectified like girls, they sometimes get ripped off and raped and then, after all that, replaced. When will bosses respect those who work for them?

Their last album was in 2009, and many of Menudo have embarked on solo careers.

Merch for Menudo included games clothing, flags, and cups. Textbook covers seem particularly clever to me! Menudo dolls (with tiny records!) were called "action figures"—a gendered differentiation marking other dolls as passive.

But the non-passive fans who followed them—such as the girls who went to every show in the beginning and who formed Menudo's first fan club, and the girls who called in to radio stations and requested their songs—indicate yet again the power of fans: they determine the success of the band. There were so many fans at the hotel where Menudo stayed that the hotel asked the band to leave.

♥♥♥

In 1978, *Cheap Trick at Budokan* introduced American teens like me—white kids who'd never left the country—to Japan in a real way. The screaming fans sounded amazing, sometimes they were louder than the band. I wanted to be at that concert. In Budokan. The pop rock punk music sounded great and had lyrics such as

Mommy's all right, Daddy's all right
They just seem a little weird

from 1978's "Surrender." My frenemy rushed over to me when the album came out, quoting those lyrics, asking if I'd heard the song and those words and the screaming fans. We knew our parents were weird and it was liberating to have that be validated by a band who was on the radio, and the fans on their song. In my eight-track player! How intimate. And universal!

Cheap Trick formed in 1973, in Illinois, all in their early to mid-twenties. Two of the band members seemed to take up most of the photo space in media and on their album covers: Singer Robin Zander and bassist Tom Petersson. Robin was the youngest, at twenty. They fit the female standard of beauty in the '70s: lean, with long hair and pretty faces. Teen pop in the '70s let males be as pretty as females. But it also insisted on it; patriarchy's beauty standards are restrictive and colonizing. Drummer Bun E. Carlos and band founder and guitarist Rick Nielsen didn't fit the standard so they weren't pictured as often.

Rick Nielsen said he wrote "Surrender" from the point of view of a teen. The lyrics are problematic in terms of race, sexuality, and gender—the song is about a parental warning of visiting a foreign land and catching a venereal disease. The lyrics use marriage and the insulting term "old maid" to define female status. I also wonder about using fans, mostly female, and from Japan, who bought tickets to the concert, whose cheers are used to further sell the band's music. What a cheap trick. But back then all I heard were the cheering fans and the words about weird parents.

As writer Shana L. Redmond told me, "Idols develop from intrigue and desire—for sexual and personal satisfaction as well as new worlds. Pop idols help us get through the day and give us something to look forward to, even if what we seek is temporary, shallow or misguided. It's not an intellectual impulse—primarily emotion and that can be thrilling."

I wonder if fandom can be as feminist as writing and playing one's own songs and instruments? Live albums by American bands in Japan made the audience part of the music, part of the experience of the album. Success beyond America validated the band as the band sought success in America. The screams of fans like the sounds of musical instruments, and therefore part of the song.

Fans validated the band. KISS dubbed in the sounds of cheering fans from different shows in Japan and the United States for 1977's *Alive II*. That they dubbed in the sound makes the band seem fake, but the band was fake, in a cartoon superhero way! The only thing KISS promised to be real was the music. And the cheering fans proved that the music was worth listening to.

Frampton Comes Alive!, a double live album by Peter Frampton in 1976, perfectly expresses interplay of band and audience; joy from musical interaction sounds so good in "Do You Feel Like We Do" that it makes this listener feel good on a blue day just to hear it.

Peter, who looked like a teen pop idol with his long golden hair and petite body clad in satin baseball jackets or country-style button-up shirts and tight pants, was born in 1950, raised in England, played guitar by age eight, had a band when he was sixteen (The Herd) whose hits made him a teen idol, then at eighteen he joined a supergroup (Humble Pie). Supergroups are bands whose members are already successful in other bands or as solo acts.

"Do You Feel Like We Do," an earlier version of which appears on an album in 1973, became a hit single from the live album in 1976. It was longer, recorded on a New York college campus in 1975, and Peter used a talk box and an effects pedal as his voice and the guitar communicated with the audience, really turning them on. It sounds so great!

But sometimes live communion can be dangerous. In 1974, fourteen-year-old Bernadette Whelan was excited about the David Cassidy concert at White City Stadium in London. She'd been saving her pocket money and talked about it with her friends, two of whom went to the concert with her. It was to be one of his last stadium shows, and 30,000 tickets sold in two days. She had his posters on her wall and her concert ticket in her hand. That May night, as she stood in adulation along with thousands of other fans, the audience stumbled into pandemonium as fans pressed forward, crushing some fans underfoot. She had a heart attack during the crush and was comatose for four days before she died. Was it because the venue did not provide seating for everyone?

Festival seating, or General Admission, at concerts is a first-come, first-serve scenario, with the earlier arrivals choosing preferred spots. At the Riverfront Coliseum in December 1979, eleven fans died in a crush at a sold-out show as the crowd surged to get inside the venue for a concert by The Who. Festival seating and not enough doors were blamed, as was the lack of enough security guards. Many of the fans who died were teens.

The Who's 1971 "Baba 'O Reilly," whose lyric "teenage wasteland" was inspired by the idea of fans traveling through wreckage to get to the concert, was also a reference to the wreckage fans left behind at concerts.

The Sex Pistols, who formed in 1975 and ended by 1978, reveled in the filth and fury. Groupie, Nancy Spungen, managed the punk rock band's bass player, Sid Vicious (her boyfriend), after the band broke up, but then she was killed at the Chelsea Hotel, with Sid under suspicion.

Punk could be dangerous with its mosh pits at concerts, too. But punk (and its mosh pits) also gave community to people who felt like outsiders. Punk rock's flyers and zines (mini-magazines, or fanzines) promoted bands in a collage style similar to teen magazines and hip-hop's sampled songs. Collaging images and words is like sampling music. The flyers and zines were personal and artistic, very individual but also communal in their casual candor and reach.

Shawna Williams was listening when her classmate, Dennis Millay, played the Sex Pistols or The Ramones on his boom box one day out in the high school smoking area. "It was kind of like somebody opened the window. It was different," Shawna told me. "It was the feeling that I got from it." What was the feeling? It was "I don't care what you say. I don't care what you think. This is me."

She'd been in love with Shaun Cassidy and his older brother, David—she loved their feathered hair, and she really loved their music. She read the teen magazines and put their centerfolds on her bedroom walls, putting new ones up every few months. Like me, she believed she had no chance to be with the idols. "I didn't fit what I thought would be loveable to them. I wasn't thin, I wasn't flat-chested, my hair didn't feather." She described herself to me as tall, Black, fat, and shy. Her mom was strict. She couldn't wear those tight shiny pants with Candie's high-heeled peep-toe mules. "I didn't look like that. I couldn't dress like that. So it was really just about the music, because that was as close as I could get. Whatever he was singing to me I felt it in my soul." The love songs soothed her. And so did punk. Shawna and I went to high school together, and we loved teen pop love songs and teen pop punk.

Rock 'n' Roll High School (1979) is a movie about a teen-aged songwriter absolutely determined to meet her favorite band so they can play her songs, Riff Randell cuts school and camps out in front of the venue to get concert tickets for everyone at her school, and when she meets the object of her adoration, they play her songs. When the principal of her high school bans the music, things blow up!

Screenwriter, Rich Whitley, grew up loving movies. A class clown whose parents discussed movies and books with him, from the Marx Brothers to Dorothy Parker, he drove his 1974 blue Dodge Dart Swinger across the country to Los Angeles to fulfill his filmmaking dream after graduating Southern Illinois University Film School. "I put everything I owned into my car, with the TV and typewriter in the front seat, of course. The two most important things."

Rich and his college friend, Russ Dvonch, a co-screenwriter of *Rock 'n' Roll High School* (and who played the character of "The Freshman" in the movie, and who gets shoved in both a locker and a filing cabinet!), took their 16 mm student films (in cans!) to Roger Corman's office at New World Pictures, where director Allan Arkush just happened to be that day.

A lifelong music collector from the suburbs of Jersey City, Allan grew up loving TV and movie soundtracks and had a toy record player. He listened to Murray the K, who had a radio show, "The Swingin' Soiree," and who was known as "the Fifth Beatle." He loved the romance of doo-wop, and he watched Dick Clark's *American Bandstand*. Allan loved music so much his parents moved the radio from the kitchen into his bedroom, which made him feel like he had a "window into the universe."

When Allan was a teen, in 1965, he found a list of must-read books in *The New York Times*. But the books were banned at Fort Lee High School, where he went. "That's … the whole impetus of the principal trying to stop their music" in *Rock 'n' Roll High School*. Teen-agers are told that what they like and what they feel is unimportant, explained Allan, who transferred the rebellious, rock 'n roll themes of films he liked such as "Shake, Rattle & Rock!" (1956) and "Rock All Night" (1957) to punk rock in his "Rock 'n' Roll High School" (1979).

The filmmakers wanted Cheap Trick or Devo, but "they wanted too much money, so we got The Ramones, who made it perfect," said Rich. The Ramones were not well known, but the band had devoted fans. The four band members wore blue jeans, white t-shirts, and black leather jackets, playing fast-paced songs based in girl-group melodies, adding nihilistic lyrics and punk rock rage. With song titles such as 1977's "Teenage Lobotomy," 1978's "I Wanna Be Sedated," "I'm Against It," and "I Just Want to Have Something to Do," the band presented a more complex and less carefree version of growing up. Against a backdrop of bricks and wearing cartoon blue, they looked like fun trouble on album covers, portraying the angry aimlessness of teen angst.

Singer and drummer Joey Ramone (b 1951), guitarist Johnny Ramone (b 1951), bassist, guitarist, and vocalist Dee Dee (b 1952), and drummer Tommy (b 1949) weren't really brothers but they met in high school and formed The Ramones in 1974, in New York City, playing 3-chord pop songs that were the basis of punk. Everyone but Tommy was born in America; Tommy was born in Hungary. Dee Dee came up with the band name, based on a Paul McCartney pseudonym. Marky (b 1952) replaced Tommy and that's who's in the movie.

The Ramones challenged conventional stereotypes of attractive men, different from most teen pop idols. But Riff Randell, the songwriting teen girl, is thin and blonde and white. How is that a challenge to tradition? "She leads the rebellion and includes everyone," Rich observed.

When Riff dreams that Joey Ramone serenades her in her bedroom, I liked that it was dreamy and fun and from the woman's point of view, but not that Riff's suddenly undressed. But P.J. Soles, who played Riff, ad-libbed a perfect teen pop line: "He looks like a poem to me."

It's Riff's best friend, the astrophysics student, Kate, who can (and does) make the bomb to blow up the school. And it's Riff who propels the plot. Riffs are powerful, driving the song (and the movie).

Blowing up a school seemed cartoonish, but they used a three-camera set-up and the editing made it look like several explosions. Rock 'n roll at its best, said Allan, is when it sounds "like the band could explode before they get to the end of the song."

But another explosion that year expressed suppression. "Ring My Bell" was number one during the summer of 1979 when Disco Demolition Night happened in Chicago. The disco hit was written by Frederick Knight for an eleven-year-old Stacy Lattisaw, but a young adult, Anita Ward (b 1956) sang it. I loved that song and I loved disco. Dances such as the Hustle and the Bump seemed like a new orientation. DJ Steve Dahl, disgruntled by a radio station that switched formats to disco at the time he was fired, asked listeners at his new station to bring their disco records to Comiskey Park stadium the night of a White Sox game in exchange for a lower ticket price and with the promise that all the records would be piled up in a dumpster and destroyed with an explosion, a promise Dahl kept. Dahl's band, Teenage Radiation, planned to play a mockery of popular disco. Incendiary, a riot ensued, with the attendant phrase, "Disco Sucks." The celebratory integrations of disco and dancing—genders, skin colors, sexual orientations—were implicitly denounced in a cruel fever.

Disco during the 1970s was a lot like Swing music in the 1940s. Marginalized groups got out on the dance floor and danced together to music made by diverse people. After Disco Demolition Night, my love of disco felt like a target.

♥ ♥ ♥

"I Was Made for Dancin'," written by Michael Lloyd, was released in 1978, from Leif Garrett's album, *Feel the Need*. Born 1961 in Hollywood, CA, Leif began as a TV actor when he was a preadolescent, and by his teens he graced teen pop mags such as *Tiger Beat* and *16*, but fan mail from girls gave money-eyed executives the idea that he could be a teen pop star. As is the trend, popular songs from yesteryears were mined for gold, and fifteen-year-old Leif covered songs that were earlier hits.

Leif a narrow column of flesh topped with abundant golden hair, his sleepytime eyes and full lips a sex appeal softened for the teens and tweens to whom he was marketed. He self-reportedly stated he lip-synced in concerts, and that he wasn't the main vocalist on his albums. His body desired by "chickenhawks" (older men who like underage boys), he said, and the millions he earned stolen from him by management.

Wonder Woman, the dark-haired blue-eyed comic book character who began in 1941 as code for fun with bondage and discipline and who represented American triumph, made her way from comics onto the TV screen from 1975 to 1979 in the popular TV show, *Wonder Woman*. Female empowerment or female objectification? Either way the fascination with females and transformation is evident in the swirl of her magical change from ordinary Diana Prince to superhero Wonder Woman. We love to watch females change clothes (odalisques! bathing beauties! beauty pageants!) or take them off (burlesque! peepholes! strippers!), and her swirl signifies the power she holds. In '70s teen pop, there is a veering of that voyeurism onto males. Teen pop idoldom was promoted by television appearances, and Leif appeared in an episode of *Wonder Woman* called "My Teenage Idol Is Missing" (September 22, 1978).

The next year, a few days before Leif's eighteenth birthday in 1979, Leif and best friend, Roland Winkler, were partying when they careened off the Hollywood freeway. They survived. Roland was paralyzed from the waist down. Leif struggled with drug addiction and alcoholism.

Today Leif is clean and sober, sometimes playing gigs. In 2016, at West Hollywood's Whiskey a Go Go, fans took over the stage as he sang "I Was Made for Dancin.'" Leif and fans sang and danced together, some fans got onstage, and then from the stage he said: "This is my exit." He told the fans that they could finish the song. And they did. Torn between following Leif, pulling at him, touching him, or the need to sing onstage, the fans (and the band) stayed onstage as Leif left.

After watching the clip, I thought, this short clip says everything about '70s teen pop: the fans make the band.

♥ ♥ ♥

My thesis at the pitch of this book was that countercultural values of feminism can be seen in the objectification of boys and men on the covers of magazines, not overt like pornography which instructs the male gaze under which women are sexually objectified, but a female gaze under which males are romantically objectified. There is a difference. Isn't there? Males were romance objects while females were sex objects. Close-ups of kissing couples in '70s romance comics were orgasmic without the dangers of sex, a moment extended in a box but not impregnating or shaming, eroticizing the female while it romanticized the male. Sexy feminism.

Sexy feminism in the 1980 film, *Foxes*, carried the '70s into the next decade with music icons Cher, Donna Summer, and Cherie Currie, and the movie's female-centered narrative predicted how teen pop would evolve: girls and women were becoming the musical powers with vast influence, clout, and money. For readers of queer subtext, the film provided a way to comment on and express desire beyond the gender binary. The world belongs to people who are bi.

However, the film normalizes underage girls having sex with adult men, then excuses it with a wedding. And is the film's opening a fetishization or an appreciation? I don't know.

Foxes opens with a slow pan up legs and arms and onto the sleeping faces of teen girls and the objects that represent them in the soft light of early morning slumber: pink hair curlers, Clearasil (skin-clearing ointment), fast food. Half-eaten Twinkies, mascara in that familiar pink and green tube, deodorant (Arm in Arm), John Travolta and KISS pictured on the wall, a driver's license with a picture of a baby in it. The alarm clock ticking. And all the while, Donna Summer sings "On the Radio" (1979), a song she wrote with Giorgio Moroder for the movie, a teen anthem about love, music, and the radio for all of us if ever there was one:

> If you think that love isn't found on the radio
> Then tune right in, you may find the love you lost

Impossible to convey the range of Donna's voice singing, and the words on the page make it smaller than the depth and span of her sound. Donna vocalizes with and beyond words.

Born 1948 in Boston, the German-speaking five-time GRAMMY award-winning singer and painter lived in Germany after she left high school early and toured in *Hair* to begin her music career. An exhibition at the GRAMMY museum in 2014–15 displayed her fine art, her original lyrics and notes, her set and fashion designs, and several of her costumes and stage clothing.

Her 1975 song, "Love to Love You Baby," gave an orgasmic soundtrack to disco, an objectification of the female form in sound, but also permission for women to enjoy sex. It's made music pornographic in a good way, though she later regretted the moans. She said she channeled singer, actor, and dancer

Marilyn Monroe while she was in the darkened studio as writer Giorgio Moroder recorded. In 1978's *Thank God It's Friday*, Donna played the part of a singer who interrupted the DJ to take the stage. After Giorgio Moroder sent the melody to her on a cassette, Donna wrote the words to "On the Radio."

In *Foxes*, the alarm interrupts the music. "Wake up," says the male DJ. "Shake your bootie," says Jodie Foster, one of the stars of the movie, referencing a disco hit by K.C. and the Sunshine band. A cat walks by the bed, and Cher next plays on the radio.

Which is how '70s teen pop began: on the radio. And in the movies. And on TV.

In the '70s, mixtapes were popular: Fans shared individual songs from various albums and artists by re-recording them onto cassettes in a labor of love. In that way, each mixtape maker was her own DJ.

It's true that radio DJs were usually men; songs on the radio were usually sung by boys and men; magazine covers usually portrayed boys and men; and music shows were usually hosted by men. Star text, like name changes, hid original identities while creating new ones, spelling out the struggle for social acceptance. But during the '70s, gender, racial, and sexual diversity could be heard and seen; the voices of females were subjective while the bodies of males were objectified; and teen pop played in multiple genres. Sexuality oriented itself variously. Signifiers of being female were worn by males— long hair, high heels, and make-up, and it was sexy. It's true that the countercultural values of feminism, racial and cultural integration, and queer activism were (and are) denounced by many, but countercultural values were also being expressed, reinforced, and furthered during '70s teen pop. The '70s teen pop idol is sometimes a tragic figure—mocked, exploited, violated, and lonely—in the quest for stardom, wealth, and musical expression. But not always.

Music amplifies the experience of being alive. And the music makes you want to fall in love! Dance! Dream!

Write a book!

What '70s teen pop represents is as important as the person who plays it. The countercultural impulses of difference and originality were being absorbed, and played back, during a '70s teen pop that made the heart throb.

Fast Forward

Teen pop stars from the '70s sometimes ended up in headline-grabbing and heartbreaking ways.

Elvis Presley died in 1977, in the bathroom of his Graceland mansion, probably from prescribed pharmaceuticals. He died when teen pop, a genre he helped create, was played by people from all over the world. Elvis dreamt of touring internationally but the furthest he got was a residency at a Las Vegas hotel with "international" in its name, and 1973's pioneering satellite concert from Hawaii. Limited by an exploitative manager, Elvis soared most in his songs, and in his afterlife. Priscilla Beaulieu Presley (b 1945), the youngster who dated Elvis Presley when she was fourteen and he was twenty-four, who married him in 1967 and bore their child, Lisa Marie (b 1968, herself a singer, and who married Michael Jackson), turned Graceland into a multi-million-dollar tourist attraction in the many years since his death, ensuring his iconic status with her shrewd business management and marketing skills. Lisa Marie died as I was writing this book. The preservation of Graceland reminds me of teen pop: a perfection that appears impervious but actually isn't. Elvis said, at the end, that he felt like an object, and it wasn't fun anymore.

The little boy sincerity was there in Elvis from the beginning, the vulnerability lifelong. His polite elasticity. The way he threw out his arms at the end of an epic song, like a little kid with a grown-up message. Elvis's swaggering insouciance was simultaneously sincere and serious, his privilege a prison. It's currently popular to make fun of Elvis as grotesque, a further signal of the destructive tendency toward mockery and exclusion rather than understanding. His image continues to be exploited.

Elvis was an artist. Can we perceive him as sonic integration moving social justice forward?

Beatle John Lennon, who promoted peace, was killed in 1980 by a fan.

Karen Carpenter died a few years later, in 1983, from complications related to her eating disorder, a suffering that began after a journalist focused on her looks instead of her music, describing her as chubby. All I have to do is look at Karen's wrecked mouth to see a little of my own. I was bulimic for years. Popular culture has yet to consistently model freedom from fatphobia.

As an undergraduate (and during some of my bulimic years), I was at work at the NYU film equipment check out desk when I heard the news Andy Gibb had died. Hedonistic, pleasure-seeking, perfectionist, Andy couldn't shake an addiction to cocaine and alcohol. Although he attained and abandoned sobriety a few times, cocaine weakened his voice and his heart. He died in 1988 at age thirty of myocarditis (an inflammation of the heart) after suffering terrible chest pains.

A punk rocker with dyed black hair in a Louise Brooks bob and a leather jacket to match was checking out some film equipment the day Andy died. I'd seen her before, hauling gear for a film she was making, and looking cooler than I'd ever seen anyone before (or since) look in person. I could never tell if she liked me. She was intimidating with her badass style and unsmiling manner, her French red lipstick and her ever-present boyfriend with the spiky hair whose short height made him seem even tougher. She walked up when I was talking about Andy's death, and I immediately thought she'd probably think

I was so uncool, baring my teen pop valentine, but I didn't censor myself. I bravely said I still loved him after all these years. With a cool toss of her head, she looked right at me, and said, "I loved him, too."

The love of a teen pop idol is extraordinarily special. It's the soft place inside.

♥ ♥ ♥

Consolidation of wealth in the 1970s contributed to the genre-building of teen pop, as has the gloss of evolving technology. MTV launched in 1981, and its televised music videos promoted bands 24/7. The music videos gave credence to teen pop, a subgenre that had been derided because of its association with female adoration, and with tweens and teens.

From the 1980s to 2020s, teen pop grew into a glossy codification that continued to play with various genres, sometimes blending the various genres of teen pop from the '70s, and sometimes making experimental music brilliantly pop. Music journalist Danyel Smith said the '80s were especially fertile for pop: "I completely and totally reject the notion that the '80s had any lack of authenticity, period. It was at the real-est."

Michael Jackson would go on to make several of the biggest-selling albums of all time, earning him the nickname the King of Pop. He turned the music video into an art form with 1982's "Thriller," the first music video inducted into the National Film Registry and among the first videos to establish MTV as a hit-making method. Fans copied his single glittery glove, his red jacket, and his dance moves. Michael also dueted with teen pop idol and former Beatle, Paul McCartney, on 1983's "Say Say Say." Michael was also twice accused of child molestation and died in 2009 of an overdose from prescribed medication.

Also disturbingly, allegations against Don Cornelius surfaced in 2022 when two Playboy Bunnies alleged that the Playboy V.I.P. locked them in his house, beating and raping them for three days. Don had previously been convicted of domestic abuse in 2008. In ill health, he committed suicide by shotgun in 2012, when he was seventy-five.

And Sweet, the band I loved so much, suffered, too. Brian looks slowly bored in promo clips over the years, and left the band in 1979. Mick died of leukemia in 2002, and Brian in 1997 from alcohol-related illnesses. Steve and Andy toured as two Sweets, touring separately and in different parts of the world, because they weren't friendly with each other anymore. Steve died in 2020.

The teen pop stars who had trouble growing up struggled with what it means to be alive on this planet, a struggle many of us can relate to: How to find pleasure that isn't harmful in this fleeting, precious, and painful life? How to be integrated, internally and in the world? It's the struggle demonstrated by a Menudo fan who prefers to stay anonymous, and who told me she was made fun of by English-speaking Americans for her love of a Spanish-singing band.

> I was a kid who loved Menudo growing up. And I was shamed for liking them because they were Spanish language and trendy. My school friends didn't know who they were because the school was mainly English speaking and American and made fun of the foreign-ness of it. It made me feel like an outsider. I hated that, but I couldn't hide my excitement about loving these beautiful musicians!

In a 2008 interview with talk show host, Oprah Winfrey, David Cassidy intently said: "The only thing that lasts, the only thing that survives, is talent." In his memoir he said he didn't want to be a teen idol. He told Oprah, "I felt very isolated and lonely." He died from alcohol-related organ failure at age sixty-six in 2017. He'd made the news again during the last years of his life, for DUIs (driving under the influence of alcohol and/or drugs) and dementia and slurred words at concerts. His mug shot rivaled that of another 1970s teen idol, Leif Garrett's. David's last words reportedly were, "So much wasted time."

♥ ♥ ♥

In the early 1980s, hip-hop and rap began their prominent airplay. Blondie's "Rapture," a song whose title references rap as does the song's name-check of graffiti artist, Fab Five Freddie, and rapper, Grandmaster Flash, combined power pop with hip-hop, and was the first rap song to reach number one on the *Billboard* charts in 1981.

Call and answer songs included U.T.F.O.'s 1984 "Roxanne, Roxanne," which was answered by a fourteen-year-old Roxanne Shanté in 1984's "Roxanne's Revenge." The Real Roxanne aka Elease Jack (b 1967) also released an answer with her 1984–85 "The Real Roxanne," in what became known as the Roxanne Wars. The latter song, with its chorus of a friend asking a question, reminds me of the girl group, the Shangri-Las.

Did you meet him at the beach?
Hells no! In the middle of December when it's twenty below?

The '80s also had the biggest pop stars selling the most records. When Janet Jackson left the control of her father and joined producers Jimmy Jam and Terry Lewis, her album, 1986's *Control*, made her an '80s pop superstar. Janet proclaims power, agency, and control in 1986's "Nasty," a song she co-wrote with Jimmy Jam and Terry Lewis. "Gimme a beat!" she demanded—and the band did. With choreography by Paula

Abdul in the video directed by Mary Lambert, teen pop here pronounces female empowerment. "No, my first name ain't baby. It's Janet. Miss Jackson if you're nasty." In the song, her last name is control.

Vocalists who put the female teen pop idol centerstage include Whitney Houston (1963–2012) and Cyndi Lauper (b 1953), who told us they wanted to dance and that girls wanted to have fun, and Brandy, who sang the theme song to a series in which she starred. Teen pop stars playing at the mall such as Debbie Gibson and Tiffany were tween-tastic. And twee pop gave indie cred to songs considered "girly" or bubblegum. After that, the dissonant charisma of art-noise band, Sonic Youth, created a daydream nation that sang about teenage riots.

Music camps, especially for girls, emerged and endured. One such school, a nonprofit founded in 1987, came from real rock roots: Fanny, the first all-girl rock group to be signed to a major label. They played on Cher's show in 1971. Two of its members, June and Jean Millington, sisters who'd been playing music since they were kids in the Philippines, formed an all-girl band in high school after they moved to America, and it eventually became Fanny and they made the charts, and then songwriter and guitarist, June, co-founded Institute for the Musical Arts with her longtime partner, Ann Hackler.

Madonna (b 1958) borrowed dance moves from gay male culture, featuring the dancing in her music videos, affirming sexual open-mindedness and cultural diversity even in the midst of a global medical crisis from HIV (human immunodeficiency virus) and AIDS (acquired immunodeficiency syndrome), a virus and its sometimes resultant disease. The epidemic was used to malign same-sex love and erotics, and it took political activism to make the reluctant medical industry to do what it's supposed to do, which is to provide healthcare.

The celebratory physicality of Prince (1958–2016) turned pop music into experimental and multi-faceted artistry—his music! His music videos! His movies! His album covers! His protest of a music label! His overt sexuality! "He was very fluid in the way he presented, always," Danyel Smith told me. Prince's music was like his self-presentation was like his art: pioneering during and after his purple reign. His death from prescribed drugs is yet another example of the dangerous pharmaceutical industry, and the revolution needed to change it.

♥ ♥ ♥

The 1990s brought more revolution. Kathleen Hanna (b 1968) co-pioneered the riot grrrl movement in the early 1990s by galvanizing a feminist fan base, many of whom were teens, with her punk band, Bikini Kill, and their punk anthem, 1992's "Rebel Girl" (produced by former Runaway, Joan Jett). Even the title of the band's 1993 debut album, *Pussy Whipped*, reverses the power from insulting girls and women to empowering them.

When Bikini Kill reunited in 2019 for their first show in twenty-two years, Kathleen began the show by extemporaneously singing a few lines a cappella from Cher's 1989 hit, "If I Could Turn Back Time" (which I filmed!). Kathleen's electro-punk band, Le Tigre, formed in 1998, recently reunited, too. Le Tigre signifies an evolving counterculture with gender non-conformity. Also, they name-check a SuperGroupie: Cynthia Plaster Caster, in 2004's "Nanny Nanny Boo Boo."

After a friend was recently introduced to Bratmobile's Allison Wolfe (b 1969), the co-originator of riot grrrl (who provided for this book the Shaun Cassidy doodle that she and her twin sister, Cindy, made in 1976), my friend looked delicate and vulnerable with awe as she told me, "Bratmobile was the first music I bought when I was 14." Her expression and experience made me think about how that kind of respectful adoration was usually reserved for teen pop males, but riot grrrl helped change that. As riot grrrls proclaimed: revolution grrrl style now! All-girl bands such as Shonen Knife (who self-released on a cassette tape), The Donnas (who handed out cassettes as a way to self-promote), and Betty Blowtorch played pop music they wrote and performed, playing all the instruments. Female-fronted bands such as No Doubt further entrenched punk in pop.

In the '90s, Selena Quintero emerged as a GRAMMY-award winning teen pop idol from Texas. Selena, whose Tejano songs popularized the Texan-Mexican music genre all over America, was raised in a protective musical family. She did her own make-up, designed her own clothes, and fell in love with her besotted guitarist. Her posthumously released song from 1995, the bilingual "Dreaming of You," expresses romantic love and the power of dreaming as lusciously as any '70s teen pop star. Selena died in 1995 at the age of twenty-three, when she was murdered by the president of her fan club. Significantly, Selena's music videos portray a teen pop idol who seemed accessible.

During the '90s, teen pop solidified as a genre with stars who began as Mouseketeers: Christina Aguilera, Selena Gomez, Britney Spears, and Justin Timberlake. Also in the 1990s, the Spice Girls commercialized feminism. Christina Aguilera and Lil' Kim made teen pop that was sexually assertive.

And a new teenybopper queen appeared in 1999 when Sonny and Cher's "The Beat Goes On" was covered by eighteen-year-old Britney Spears on her 1999 teen dare of a debut album, … *Baby One More Time*, the biggest-selling album ever recorded by a teen girl, and who embodied and codified the teen pop ideal as an athletic expression of performance that signified prowess and a strict code of allowable sexuality, singing in a voice that combined little-girl inflection with adult woman sophistication. Britney's later struggle for autonomy from her father's legal control could be read as the trouble with patriarchy.

Boy bands such as Backstreet Boys, Boyz II Men, and BTS demonstrated teen pop's continued music-making, diversity, and fandom, and some yielded idols such as Bobby Brown from New Edition; Ricky Martin, the King of Latin Pop, from Menudo; Justin Timberlake from *NSYNC; and Harry Styles from One Direction. Even the nickname for fans of teen pop solo star, Justin Bieber, indicates the adoration of teen pop music and their idols: Beliebers.

And in the 1990s, teen magazines such as *Sassy* (b 1988) promoted a way of being that seemed more real, sloppier, and jagged and ambitious, promoting feminism and riot grrrl and women in music. Hole's Courtney Love and Nirvana's Kurt Cobain were a punk rock dream come true when the two musicians made the cover of *Sassy* in 1992 as a smooching couple in love, each with their own band and grunge glamour. *Bust* (b 1993) and *bitch* (b 1996) started as zines. DIY (do-it-yourself) went online with *Rookie* (b 2011), whose contributors were often actual teens. The editors and writers were female, not males posing as teen girls. Teen magazines, which had offered a way for the female gaze to actually and with desire look at males, encouraged the female gaze to look beyond them.

Beyoncé (b 1981), the teen pop star with all-female Destiny's Child at the turn of the century, grew up into her own superstardom in the early twenty-first century, creating popular music that seemed like a superpower with her genre-expanding self-empowering reach. Queen Bey is teen pop all grown up.

♥ ♥ ♥

Miley Cyrus, who'd starred as a teen in *Hannah Montana*, a TV show from 2006 to 2011 about a pop star, gave a performance at the 2013 Video Music Awards that was publicly criticized as racist and sexist. But currently, in the early 2020s, teen pop stars such as Billie Eilish (b 2001) represent a new way of presenting girls and women: bodies covered in slouchy clothes; hair dyed in many colors like green, blonde, and/or black; finger painting emotion on the face; and long pointed fake fingernails create a refusal of gendered construction. But her voice—sexualized and soft like a baby's sophisticated coo shaped by mourning, like being enveloped in sad clouds—sings songs with mature awareness of emotion and desire. Olivia Rodrigo (b 2003), who sings about being old enough to drive, makes the experience of heartbreak sound and look a lot like getting over it.

Harry Styles (b 1994), legs spread, cocks his head and holds out a friendly blue flower in place of his penis, a contemporary teen idol on the cover of *Rolling Stone* in 2022, photographed by Amanda Fordyce for an article written by Brittany Spanos. In the photo layout inside, Harry on the couch under multi-colored boas, a lavender sweater vest opened, a cross on his bare chest, and the sun soft through a billowing curtain behind him, offers an odalisque for the new Age of the Unicorn: a mythical teen ideal all grown up, sexually experienced. sexually integrated, sexually experimental, someone who'd be your friend after. Flirtatious, theatrical, casual.

By 2022, documentaries became the new promotional tools for young teen pop stars who haven't even died yet, proliferating on streaming services. The teen pop idol, Selena Gomez (b 1992), who began on the Disney show, eventually performing hit songs and starring in a binge-worthy TV series she executive produced, made a documentary that created an aesthetics of mental illness. Maddeningly savvy!

The internet and social media have proven more than necessary in a pandemic era; they are vital. By 2020, another virus provided an obstacle to the abandonment of the '70s: COVID. But musicians toured online, and fans sang and danced along. As of this writing in 2022, social media has allowed teens to become influencers with their own platforms.

Social media furthered progressive change in a counterculture gone digital. In the early 2000s, activist Tarana Burke founded the MeToo movement, and in 2017, actor Alyssa Milano posted it as a hashtag, sparking a viral campaign. #MeToo fights sexual assault and rape culture. Filmmakers such as dream hampton brought #MeToo to the music industry.

Countercultural values of feminism, civil rights, queer activism, and cultural integration in a capitalism going amok resulted in the teen pop of today, in which females and people of color can earn as much as or more than white males, and grace magazine covers without being mostly naked, or always sexually objectified, or held to a gender-based social construct of heterosexuality. A teen pop star today builds an empire, and is more likely to run it, too. Jazz and big bands were named after the usually male bandleaders, not the female singers; but today the names of female singers in any genre are usually known. And sometimes the women singers are so powerful that they are called divas, a term that signals the power it tries to dismiss.

Why do we create pop stars? Because we are a "society of spectacle," music journalist Evelyn McDonnell explained to me. As I wrote this book—and edited out more than half of it because of word count restraints—I realized that teen pop stars are representations of an individual's struggle to be treated with respect as well as representing a group or genre's struggle to respectfully co-exist. Whether that group is based on race, gender, sexuality, culture, or the band itself, how do we once and for all stop oppression, abuse, and exploitation? Plus, pretty person privilege and ableism overwhelmed me. I'm hoping Lady Gaga, Lizzo, Katy Perry, Blackpink, and Taylor Swift, just to name a few more of the teen pop powerhouses, will influence a new wave of social progress in which more people can earn a sustainable and flourishing living doing what they love.

I'm hoping that today's teen pop stars aren't representing a global gender-fluid rainbow of just another elite group of people who thrive, because then the power structure hasn't really changed, only the places of a few people in it.

In sixth grade in 1977, the first day of music class, we chose our instruments. They were in a big pile—flutes, clarinets, a few trumpets and trombones, some saxophones, the drums, some cymbals. Almost everyone ran so fast to the pile, pushing and elbowing each other out of the way and climbing over each other to get to the one instrument they wanted.

I dare the playback of real counterculture to make room for us all, singing mutual respect and shared profit, individual authenticity, and unique creative expression. Our true counterculture has a generous heart.

10 Essential Tracks

Jackson 5ive, "ABC" 1970

The Partridge Family, "I Woke Up in Love This Morning" 1971

The DeFranco Family, "Heartbeat (It's a Lovebeat)" 1973

MFSB featuring The Three Degrees, theme song from Soul Train "T.S.O.P. (The Sound of Philadelphia)" 1973

Bay City Rollers, "Saturday Night" 1973–76

The Runaways, "Cherry Bomb" 1976

Sweet, "Love Is Like Oxygen" 1978

Andy Gibb, "Waiting for You" 1978

Blondie, "Dreaming" 1979

Donna Summer, "On the Radio" 1979

Pause

For my mom, Lucretia Baldwin "Teka" Ward, my brother, Lacey Thomas Smith, Jr., and my partner, Wayne Earl Pemberton, Jr. You are the stars in my eyes. Thank you for your time, which is so precious. Thank you for believing in me. You've always encouraged my writing and art-making, and I am so very grateful. Thank you for your editorial guidance in the eleventh hour! Thank you to my father, Lacey Smith, Sr., for always affirming my writing, and for that first typewriter when I was 16!

Thank you to my friends, Lucie Vaughn and Natalee Woods. You each gave such loving, practical, and insightful support to me as I wrote this book. Deep appreciation to my friend, Judy Ornelas Sisneros, who insisted I hit up 33 1/3 one more time. Thank you to my friend, Grace Krilanovich, who first suggested I apply to 33 1/3 so many years ago. Thanks to all of you for your editorial guidance in the eleventh hour, too!

Shout-outs to my forever friends: Mary Yates, my bestie from childhood; Aimee Nabors, my best friend when we were tweens and teens; Nadine B., my real friend from the rooms; Debbie, my Swans sister from riot grrrl Los Angeles; and Dennybird, the first true musician I ever met.

Wayne, thank you for the idea to write about teen pop! Thank you to everyone who talked with me about teen pop! Thank you to Alice Bag and Allison Wolfe for the photos!

Thank you to everyone at 33 1/3, Bloomsbury and Integra for being so kind, and so patient with me, and for letting me have a voice in decisions. I first applied to 33 1/3 in 2006, and applied two more times after that, and was so thrilled when you contacted me in 2020 to write a book for your new series. It's been very special and meaningful, one of the best things in my life, and I'll never forget it.

Mom, thank you for editing my proposal, for your feminism, and for your love of music.

Thank you to the musicians and music-makers. ♥

Record

This bibliography refers to those I quoted or paraphrased in my book.

Liner Notes:

Barth, Lori. Personal interview. 10.16.18.

Berrigan, Don. Personal interview. 9.27.18; 10.4.18; 1.20.19.

Des Barres, Pamela. Personal interviews, texts and conversations from 2012 to 2022.

Diltz, Henry. Personal interview. 7.15.20.

Mockingbird, Taquila. Personal interview. 10.11.19.

Plaster Caster, Cynthia. Personal interviews. 2.4.12; 10.24.13.

Rolfe, Karen, and Jennie Rosenthal. Personal interviews. 3.28.22.

Rewind:

The Andrews Sisters. "Bei Mir Bistu Shein." 1937.

Berrigan, Don. Personal interview. 9.27.18; 10.4.18; 1.20.19.

Berry, Chuck. "Roll Over Beethoven." 1956.

Des Barres, Pamela. Personal interviews, texts and conversations from 2012 to 2022.

Dister, Alan. *The Story of Rock: Smash Hits and Superstars.* New York: Harry N. Abrams, Inc., 1993. Print.

Elvis Presley: The Searcher. Directed by Tom Zimny. USA: HBO Documentary Films, 2018.

Gardner, Ava. *Ava: My Story.* The United States and Canada: Bantam Books, 1990.

Good Ol' Freda. Directed by Ryan White. USA: Magnolia Pictures, 2013.

Gore, Lesley. "You Don't Own Me." 1963.

Hamill, Pete. *Why Sinatra Matters.* New York: Little, Brown and Company, Hachette Book Group, 1998. (p 53)

Hitsville: The Making of Motown. Directed by Ben Turner and Gabe Turner. USA: Showtime Networks, 2019.

How the Beatles Changed the World. Directed by Tom O'Dell. USA: Vision Films, 2017.

"Interview with Darlene Love (The Blossoms)." *Elvis Australia: Official Elvis Presley Fan Club.* Interview by Michael Musto for *Village Voice.* 8.9.18. https://www.elvis.com.au/presley/interview-with-darlene-love-the-blossoms.shtml Digital link. Accessed June, 2022.

Jazz. "Gumbo: Beginnings to 1917." "Our Language: 1924–9." "The True Welcome: 1929–34." "Swing: Pure Pleasure: 1935–7." "Swing: the Velocity of Celebration: 1937–9." "Dedicated to Chaos 1940–5." "Risk 1945–55." "The Adventure 1955–60." "A Masterpiece by Midnight 1961–Present." Directed by Ken Burns. USA: Florentine Films, 2001.

Little Richard. "Tutti Frutti." 1955.

Louis Armstrong's Black & Blues. Directed by Sacha Jenkins. USA: Apple Original Films, 2022.

Mahon, Maureen. *Black Diamond Queens: African American Women and Rock and Roll*. Durham: Duke University Press, 2020. (pp 40–1)

Plaster Caster, Cynthia. Personal interviews. 2.4.12; 10.24.13.

Roxon, Lillian. *Rock Encyclopedia*. USA: A Grosset & Dunlap Original Universal Library Edition, 1971. (pp 212–13)

Rumble: The Indians Who Rocked the World. Directed by Catherine Bainbridge and Alfonso Maiorana. USA: Rezolution Pictures, 2017.

Server, Lee. *Ava Gardner: "Love Is Nothing."* New York: St. Martin's Press, 2006. (p 180, p 265)

Sinatra: All or Nothing at All. Directed by Alex Gibney. USA: Jigsaw Productions, 2015.

Smith, Danyel with Daphne Brooks. "Shine Bright: A Very Personal History of Black Women in Pop." *Popular Music Books in Process Series*. 4.12.22. (27:11) https://www.youtube.com/watch?v=kl_B9PRndN0 Digital link. Accessed January, 2023.

Vanilla, Cherry. Personal interviews. 4.26.12; 12.13.16; 12.20.16; 6.14.18.

Play:

ABBA. "Dancing Queen." 1976.

"Andy Gibb." *A & E Biography*. https://youtu.be/2_O5sehuRLc Digital link. Accessed October, 2022.

Armendariz, Alicia. Personal interviews. 10.7.20; 10.28.20; 2.18.23.

Bag, Alice. *Violence Girl: East L.A. Rage to Hollywood Stage, a Chicana Punk Story*. USA: Feral House, 2011.

"Bay City Rollers." *Behind the Music*. 8.21.99. https://youtu.be/3bCEQUPtyz4 Digital link. Accessed October, 2022.

Blondie. "Heart of Glass." 1978.

Bowie, David. "Space Oddity." 1969.

Bowie, David. "Rebel Rebel." 1974.

Cassidy, David. *Could It Be Forever? My Story*. Great Britain: Headline Publishing Group, 2007.

Cheap Trick. "Surrender." 1978.

Chic. "Le Freak." 1978.

Currie, Cherie and Neal Shusterman. *Neon Angel the Cherie Currie Story*. Los Angeles: Price Stern Sloan, 1989. (pp 27–30)

"David Cassidy." *Behind the Music*. 12.20.98. https://www.youtube.com/watch?v=PWCLou1XeKc Digital link. Accessed September, 2022.

DeFranco, Tony. *Your TV History*. "Tony and Benny DeFranco Come Home to Port Colburne." November, 2001. (6:01) https://youtu.be/W5xJud6TaBA Digital link. Accessed February 18, 2023.

Diltz, Henry. Personal interview. 7.15.20.

"Donny & Marie." *Behind the Music*. August 22, 1999. https://www.youtube.com/watch?v=jD3ZT2dRNLA Digital link. Accessed October, 2022.

"DUI's and Dementia: Inside David Cassidy's Secret Battle." *Dr Phil*. March 1, 2017. https://youtu.be/t-bycDOhZ2g Digital link. Accessed September, 2022.

Edgeplay: A Film about the Runaways. Directed by Victory Tischler—Blue. USA: Sacred Dogs Entertainment, 2004.

Foxes. Directed by Adrian Lyne. USA: Casablanca Filmworks or PolyGram Pictures,1980.

Fried, Stephen. *Thing of Beauty: The Tragedy of Supermodel Gia*. New York: Pocket Books, 1993. (pp 30–1)

Garrett, Leif. "I Was Made for Dancing." Filmed by Jake Perry. 11.12.16. https://youtu.be/5fD6-4eAgHQ Digital link. Accessed October, 2022.

Garrett, Leif. Studio 10. https://youtu.be/YR7cWlgSGCl Digital link. Accessed October, 2022.

"Good Morning Britain." *Radio X*. 5.25.19. https://www.radiox.co.uk/news/tv-film/elton-john-ex-fiance-linda-hannon-not-in-rocketman/ Digital link. Accessed August 2, 2022.

H., Kate. "David Cassidy: A Brief and Belated Eulogy." *Medium*. 2.5.18. https://medium.com/@tallmank9/david-cassidy-a-brief-and-belated-eulogy-80e77b4dbd9d

Harry, Debbie. "1975." *Behind the Music*. May 6, 2001. https://youtu.be/nEY1HhdzNpY Digital link. Accessed October, 2022.

Hart, Bruce and Carole. *Sooner or Later*. NYC: Avon Books, 1978.

Heart. "Dreamboat Annie." 1975.

Hills, Megan C. "Remember When Elvis Presley's White Jumpsuits Changed How Men Dressed Forever?" *CNN Style*. Updated June 22, 2022. https://www.cnn.com/style/article/elvis-presley-fashion-remember-when/index.html Digital link. Accessed March, 2022.

The Jackson 5ive. "ABC." 1970.

Jasmine, Lucretia Tye. "Morgana Welch, A Queen of L.A." 10.22.18. https://pleasekillme.com/morgana-welch/

Jasmine, Lucretia Tye. "Star Magazine for Foxy Teens, A 1970s 'Groupie' Magazine." 1.14.19. https://pleasekillme.com/star-magazine/

Jasmine, Lucretia Tye. "Cult Classic 'Rock 'N Roll High School' Celebrates 40th Anniversary with Lush Restoration and Interviews with the Filmmakers." 12.26.19. https://thelosangelesbeat.com/2019/12/cult-classic-rock-n-roll-high-school-celebrates-40th-anniversary-with-lush-restoration-and-interviews-with-the-filmmakers/

Jones, Davy. "Girl." 1970–1971.

"Karen Carpenter: When I Was Sixteen." *Star*. Interview by Nancy Hardwick. March, 1973. (pp 16–17)

KISS. "C'mon and Love Me." 1975.

"Kool Herc Merry-Go-Round Technique." https://youtu.be/7qwml-F7zKQ Digital link. Accessed August, 2022.

Led Zeppelin. "Sick Again." 1975.

Menudo: Forever Young. Directed by Ángel Manuel Soto. USA: Muck Media, 2022.

Moses, Ann. "Meet Marie Osmond." *Ann Moses*. https://annmoses.com/meet-marie-osmond/ Digital link. Accessed September, 2022.

Moses, Ann. Personal interview. 12.7.22.

National Public Radio. "There Was Nothing Like 'Soul Train' On TV. There's Never Been Anything Like It Since." *It's Been a Minute*. 9.28.21. https://www.npr.org/2021/09/14/1037118049/soul-train-hanif-abdurraqib Digital link. Accessed August, 2022.

Osmond, Donny. "Puppy Love." 1972.

Parliament. "Flash Light." 1978.

The Partridge Family. "One Night Stand." 1971.

Powers, Ann. *Good Booty: Love and Sex, Black and White, Body and Soul in American Music*. New York: HarperCollins Publishers, 2017. (p 148)

Quatro, Suzi. Personal interview. 6.24.22.

Redmond, Shana L. Personal interview. 11.13.22.

"Rex Reveals: 'My Love Is the Only Thing I Have to Give.'" *Teen Beat*. August, 1980. https://www.12stringbass.net/teen-beat-magazine Digital link. Accessed October, 2022.

Rhymes, Shameika. "Cynthia Horner Is Breathing New Life into Right On! Magazine." 10.17.18. https://www.shondaland.com/live/a23696502/right-on-magazine/ Digital link. Accessed November, 2022.

Rock 'n' Roll High School. Directed by Allan Arkush and Joe Dante. USA: New World Pictures, 1979.

Rolfe, Karen. Personal interview. 9.19.22.

Rolfe, Karen and Jennie Rosenthal. Personal interviews. 3.28.22 and 4.4.22.

The Runaways. "Cherry Bomb." 1976.

The Runaways. "Saturday Night Special." 1978.

Ryan, Gary. "Debbie Harry on a Life Like No Other: 'I Have a Stubborn Will to Survive.'" *NME*. 10.2.19. https://www.nme.com/features/debbie-harry-face-it-autobiography-70s-bowie-feminism-2552924 Digital link. Accessed October, 2022.

Sherman, Bobby. "Waiting at the Bus Stop." 1971.

Smith, Danyel. Personal interview. 6.27.22.

Sonny & Cher. "The Beat Goes On." 1967.

Spence, Simon. *When the Screaming Stops: The Dark History of the Bay City Rollers*. USA: Omnibus Press, 2016.

Spungen, Deborah. *And I Don't Want to Live This Life*. USA: Ballantine Books, 1983.

Star. Issues February—June. Los Angeles: Petersen Publishing Company, 1973.

Steinem, Gloria. *Revolution from Within: A Book of Self-Esteem*. USA: Little, Brown and Company, 1992. (p 89)

Summer, Donna. "On the Radio." 1979.

Sweet. "Love Is Like Oxygen." 1978.

The Who. "Baba 'O Reilly." 1971.

Travolta, John. "Greased Lightnin'." 1978.

Vanilla, Cherry. Personal interview. 10.31.22.

Vaughn, Lucie. Personal interview. 7.3.22.

Vincentelli, Elisabeth. *ABBA Gold*. USA: Continuum, 2004. (p 17)

Wald, Gayle. Personal interview. 5.2.22.

Williams, Shawna. Personal interview. 3.22.22.

Wilson, Ann and Nancy with Charles R. Cross. *Kicking & Dreaming: A Story of Heart, Soul, and Rock & Roll*. USA: It Books, 2012. (p 44)

Fast Forward:

"David Cassidy, The Cosby Kids." *The Oprah Winfrey Show*. Chicago. February 12, 2008. https://www.youtube.com/watch?v=5JaTV0M_0Tc. Accessed 15.09.22.

Jackson, Janet. "Nasty." 1986.

McDonnell, Evelyn. Personal interview. 11.7.22.

Melnick, Lynn and Deborah Paredez. "Sequins & Survival: On Dolly Parton, Selena, and the American Diva." *Popular Music Books in Process Series*. February 13, 2023. 21:20 minutes onwards. https://youtu.be/1fX6rlgxvyU. Accessed 2.23.23.

Roxanne with U.T.F.O. "The Real Roxanne." 1984.

Smith, Danyel. Personal interview. 6.27.22.

Stop/Eject

1970s Teen Pop cassette drawing by Lucretia Tye Jasmine.